THE BURGER CHEF
MURDERS
IN INDIANA

Julie Young

D1599062

THE
History
PRESS

Published by The History Press
Charleston, SC
www.historypress.com

Copyright © 2019 by Julie Young
All rights reserved

Cover images from newspapers.com.

First published 2019

Manufactured in the United States

ISBN 9781467143080

Library of Congress Control Number: 2019935364

To Jayne, Ruth, Daniel and Mark…The truth is out there.

CONTENTS

ACKNOWLEDGEMENTS

A s an author, I have learned that every book has its difficulties, but this one was particularly challenging. I knew going into it that I would not solve the forty-year mystery, nor was that my intent. I merely wanted to examine the known facts of the Burger Chef murder case, the strange series of events leading up to it and the tireless efforts of the law enforcement officers who investigated the incident over the last four decades.

I could not have done it without the love and support of my husband, Shawn, and our two sons, Chris and Vincent, who understood when I was in the "zone" and unable to concentrate on anything else. Thank you for listening as I riddled out the facts, speculated and fell down numerous rabbit holes in an effort to connect the dots. You are the best, and I love you all very much.

Thank you to fellow authors John McDonald and Scott Sanders for their assistance with images, as well as Kyle Brown, administrator of the Burger Chef Memories website. I could not have finished this project without your help, and I truly appreciate it. I also want to acknowledge John Rodrigue and the staff of The History Press who were enthusiastic about this project from the start and were willing to entrust me with such sensitive subject matter. Thank you for believing in me!

To Steve Barnett at the Irvington Historical Society: thank you for working your magic on the manuscript. Your edits make my work better, and I always feel better when I know you have given it the once-over. What would I ever do without you?

And finally, thank you to all of my readers and friends who heard about this project and encouraged me throughout the writing process. Your support means everything to me, and I hope the end result lives up to your expectations.

AUTHOR'S NOTE

There are few dates in my life that I can account for forty years later, but I can honestly say that I know exactly where I was and what I was doing on the evening of November 17, 1978. I was at home in my pajamas watching *The Star Wars Holiday Special*—a piece of television history that was so awful, it only aired the one time.

Like legions of kids across the country (and throughout the world), I became obsessed with the sci-fi classic from the moment it hit the big screen in May 1977, and I remember a time when there was only one place to find memorabilia tied to the movie: at my local Burger Chef restaurant.

Burger Chef was the brainchild of Frank and Donald Thomas, who patented a flame broiler for their parent company, the General Equipment Corporation, before opening their first restaurant at 1300 West Sixteenth Street in Indianapolis in the spring of 1958. An upscale version of Burger King, Burger Chef was a big hit thanks in part to its burger-fries-and-drink combination meal, which sold for forty-five cents. The chain spread quickly, and throughout the 1960s, Burger Chef stores could be found in thirty-eight states across the United States, and it was one of the most beloved fast-food chains in the country.

By the early 1970s, the chain peaked with 1,200 stores and was second only to McDonald's in terms of popularity. Customers flocked to the double burger known as the "Big Shef"; the "Works Bar," which enabled folks to customize their sandwiches; and a kids' meal that featured colorful characters such as Burger Chef and Jeff; Count Fangburger, the vampire; and Cackleburger, the witch.

In addition to developing the original "Funmeal," Burger Chef was one of the first fast-food entities to partner with a movie studio in order to offer merchandise tied to an upcoming film. While these kinds of licensing deals are commonplace today, when Burger Chef announced its partnership with 20th Century Fox and its then unknown *Star Wars* film, it was an unheard-of concept. However, it proved to be very lucrative. The initial offering was a free *Star Wars* poster with the purchase of a large Coke, but the campaign eventually grew to include a *Star Wars*–themed Funmeal box, collectible glasses and other giveaways that few *Star Wars* fans would pass up—especially at a time when *Star Wars* merchandise was hard to find.

Burger Chef was not only a popular place to eat and score *Star Wars* swag, but it was also a popular place to work, especially if you were a high school student looking to make a few bucks after school. With eight hundred locations across the Midwest and southern states in the late 1970s, still second only to the Golden Arches, most everyone knew someone who worked at a Burger Chef. Sure, they were primarily entry-level positions, but kids got their foot in the door, learned new skills and were able to save for their education or that first set of wheels.

But in November 1978, the storied history of Burger Chef took a dark turn. While I was safe at home watching the *Star Wars* gang celebrate "Life Day," four kids across town were getting ready to close their Burger Chef restaurant for the night.

It was to be the last night of their lives.

NAMES ASSOCIATED WITH THE BURGER CHEF MURDER CASE

(In order of appearance)

Daniel Davis, sixteen: Crew member at the Speedway Burger Chef who was murdered on November 17, 1978

Jayne Friedt, twenty: Assistant manager at the Speedway Burger Chef who was murdered on November 17, 1978

Carolyn Friedt: Mother of Jayne Friedt

Ed Cherne: Area manager for Burger Chef in 1978

Ruth Ellen Shelton, seventeen: Crew member at the Speedway Burger Chef who was murdered on November 17, 1978

Rachel Shelton: Ruth Ellen Shelton's mother

John Shelton: Ruth Ellen Shelton's father

Mark Flemmonds, sixteen: Crew member at the Speedway Burger Chef who was murdered on November 17, 1978

Robert Flemmonds: Father of Mark Flemmonds

Blondell Flemmonds: Mother of Mark Flemmonds

Robert Gilyeat: Speedway Burger Chef store manager

Brian Kring: Former employee of the Speedway Burger Chef

William Crafton: Speedway police lieutenant

Julia Scyphers: Speedway resident who was murdered in her garage on July 26, 1978

Fred Scyphers: Husband of Julia Scyphers

Brett Kimberlin: The man charged with the Speedway bombing incident in September 1978

Sandra Barton: Julia Scyphers's daughter who was employed by Brett Kimberlin

William Bowman: An associate of Brett Kimberlin who is believed to be the man who murdered Julia Scyphers in her garage on July 26, 1978

Michael Grider: 1973 Speedway High School graduate and resident

George Friedt: Father of Jayne Friedt

Buddy Ellwanger: Speedway police officer

Fred Heger: Johnson County resident who owned the wooded property where the bodies of the Burger Chef crew members were found

Rosemary Heger: Wife of Fred Heger

Jim Cramer: Indiana State Police lieutenant who was called in to help with the Burger Chef investigation in November 1978

Richard "Dick" Tudor: Johnson County coroner in 1978

Harley Palmer: Former Johnson County coroner who conducted the autopsies on the bodies of the Burger Chef murder victims

Tom Pritchard: Johnson County sheriff in 1978

Doran Miller: Johnson County deputy sheriff in 1978.

Brook Appleby: Indiana State Police investigator

Larry Myers: Owner of a private ambulance service in Johnson County who was hired to remove the bodies of the four victims from the Heger property

Mark Myers: Son of Larry Myers who helped remove the bodies of the victims from the Heger property

Reverend Russell Blowers: Minister at the 91st Street Christian Church

Anthony Etienne: Principal of Decatur Central High School

Bruce Roaden: Daniel Davis's best friend

Reverend Jack McCormick: Ruth Ellen Shelton's pastor

William Hendricks: Minister at the Avon Christian Church

Edward Smooth, elder at the Eagle Creek Congregation of Jehovah's Witness

John Bainbridge: Principal of Speedway High School

Ginger Haggard: Burger Chef employee who traded shifts with Mark Flemmonds on November 17, 1978

George Gale: Principal of Northwest High School

William Mahler: Lieutenant with the Marion County Sheriff's Department

Robin England: Ball State art student who created the clay models of the men seen behind the Burger Chef on November 17, 1978

Robert Allen: Indiana State Police major

Danny White: Possible suspect arrested in Chicago who was later cleared of any involvement in the Burger Chef murders

Danny Minigh: Possible suspect arrested in Chicago who was later cleared of any involvement in the Burger Chef murders

Richard Bolinger: Burger Chef spokesperson

William Hudnut III: Mayor of Indianapolis in 1978

Stephen Goldsmith: Marion County prosecutor

Ken York: Indiana State Police investigator

Richard Bumps: Indiana State Police detective

Charles D. Gantz: Johnson County prosecutor

Virgil Vandagriff: Sergeant with Marion County Sheriff's Department

Joseph Eke: President of the Metropolitan Board of Police Commissioners

Robert Copeland: Speedway Police chief at the time that the Burger Chef murders occurred

William Burgan: Speedway Police captain who replaced Robert Copeland as interim police chief after Copeland was fired

W. Sherrill Alspauch: Speedway evidence technician

Ronald L. Bruce: Speedway detective

Terry Collinsworth: Indiana State Police trooper assigned to Johnson County

Barry Turner: Indiana State Police trooper who was assigned to Johnson County

Lloyd Monroe: Indiana State Police captain

Don Lindsay: Indiana State Police trooper

Leon Griffith: Indiana State Police sergeant

John Hruban: Member of the Indianapolis Police Department

Buddy Ellwanger: Lieutenant with the Speedway Police Department

Carold Baker: Sergeant with the Marion County Sheriff's Department

Timothy Piccione: Possible suspect known for robbing two Burger Chef locations in July 1978

John W. Defibaugh: Possible suspect known for robbing two Burger Chef locations in July 1978

James W. Friedt: Brother of Jayne Friedt who was charged with selling thirty grams of cocaine

Larry Charmichael: Lieutenant with the Speedway Police Department

Kevin M. Flemmonds: Brother of Mark Flemmonds who was convicted of the robbery and murder of Adrian A. Brown

William "Stoney" Vann: Indiana State Police trooper who inherited the Burger Chef case in 1998

Dan Luzadder: Reporter with the *Indianapolis Star* newspaper

Donald Ray Forrester: Inmate who confessed to have played a role in the Burger Chef murders

Betty "Ray" Forrester: Donald Ray Forrester's mother

Donald Forrester: Donald Ray Forrester's father

Everett Decker: Inmate at the Indiana State Reformatory

Morris Hammelman: Prison counselor at the Indiana State Reformatory

David Molnar: Inmate at the Indiana State Reformatory

Sylvester Brown: Inmate at the Indiana State Reformatory

Chris Cloud: Marion County Sheriff's Deputy

Mel Willsey: Detective with the Marion County Sheriff's Department

Paul Simons: Detective with the Marion County Sheriff's Department

Reece Townsend, DDS: A local dentist who was involved in prison ministry and took an interest in Donald Ray Forrester's case

Steve Sherman: A local attorney who was involved in prison ministry and took an interest in Donald Ray Forrester's case

Gary Maxey: A narcotics officer with the Marion County Sheriff's Department who worked on the Burger Chef case in the mid-1980s

Robert Yarnell: A detective with the Marion County Sheriff's Department who worked on the Burger Chef case in the mid-1980s

David Cook: Marion County chief trial deputy

Cloid Shuler: Department of Corrections deputy commissioner

Allen Pruitt: Was across the street from the Crawfordsville Road Burger Chef on November 17, 1978, and purportedly saw the crew members being taken from the restaurant just prior to their deaths

Jake Query: Radio host who sponsored a fund drive to supply a headstone for Mark Flemmonds's grave

Chapter 1

AN EXCEPTIONAL CREW

The evening of November 17, 1978, was just like any other Friday night for the four young crew members closing the Burger Chef Restaurant at 5725 Crawfordsville Road in Speedway, Indiana. After serving up Big Shefs, Funmeals and other signature fare to their customers, the employees locked the doors at 11:00 p.m. and began to clean the store in preparation for the following day. Nothing seemed amiss as Daniel Davis, sixteen, changed out of his brown and orange uniform shirt in the restroom while his assistant manager, Jayne Friedt, twenty, took the cash from the register drawers and placed it in the safe located in the manager's office.

Jayne's career with the fast-food franchise began when she was a seventeen-year-old student at Avon High School. She started working for Burger Chef at the 38th Street and Lafayette Road location before transferring to the Speedway store in the spring of 1978. Everyone who encountered the longhaired dimpled young lady known as "Sweet Jayne" said she was a happy person who was always ready to tell or laugh at a joke.

"She had a zany smile that always reminded me of Lily Tomlin because when she smiled, her eyes would crinkle up into these crescent moon shapes," said Lori Shufflebarger, who was a year behind Jayne in high school and frequently ate lunch with her at the same table in the cafeteria.

Jayne was a well-rounded individual who was involved in a number of activities while holding down her part-time job. She was involved with her school's yearbook staff, concert band, choir, pep club, drama, gymnastics and more. She also served as a teacher's aide and library assistant—supervisory positions that no doubt helped her succeed in the workplace. And although she took her managerial job seriously, she was a professional who had the ability to get beyond the small stuff in order to get her work done.

Jayne's professionalism and work ethic did not go unnoticed. Three months after her transfer to the Speedway Burger Chef, she was promoted to assistant manager. It was a validation for the young woman who hoped to rise through the company's corporate structure but was often overlooked when it came to advancement opportunities.

"She fought hard to get her promotion," Jayne's mother, Carolyn Friedt, said. "She always talked about how young boys she trained…received promotions ahead of her. Then management realized what a good worker she was and made her an assistant manager."

Ed Cherne, area manager for Burger Chef, said Jayne more than proved herself on the job. At the age of twenty, she was logging approximately fifty-two hours a week, and when she was at the store, she ran the entire operation. She hired new employees, trained crew members, took inventory, handled money and more. She worked easily with those who were getting used to their first afterschool job as well as seasoned employees who were twice her age.

"I can't really say enough about Jayne," said Cherne. "She was always so happy and so darned optimistic. Whenever I'd walk through the restaurant with a frown on my face, she'd say, 'You're not smiling today!' How could someone like that miss?"

As Jayne led the others through their nightly procedure, she was unaware that she was in line to receive another promotion—this time to the position of store manager. It was quite a coup to be one of the youngest managers in the company, but she'd earned it. By January, it was possible that Jane would be in charge of her own store, and her current boss couldn't wait to give her the good news.

Like Jayne, Ruth Ellen Shelton, seventeen, was a poised and professional young lady who was in the fall of her junior year at Northwest High School. When she wasn't clearing the "Works Bar" or wiping down Formica tables in the Burger Chef dining room after hours, she was an honor student who took the STEM-related classes that girls in the late 1970s typically shied away from. But Ruth Ellen was far from a typical teenager. That November, she was pursuing a double major in business and math in hopes that her heavy course load would help her get into a good college, where she planned to earn a degree in the emerging field of computer science.

Illustration from a Burger Chef employee hygiene manual depicting nightly cleaning procedures. This literature was distributed to crew members in the 1970s. *Author's private collection.*

Classmates said Ruth Ellen was a quiet, studious and creative girl, and when she was not working, hitting the books or engaging in her latest macramé project, she studied voice at Indiana Central University (today the University of Indianapolis) and was active in a variety of youth ministries at the Westside Church of the Nazarene.

"She often talked about how much fun she was having with her fellowship group," Ruth Ellen's mother, Rachel Shelton, said. "They were studying the Book of Revelation, and she was really fascinated by that."

Like other girls her age, Ruth Ellen alternately teased and mentored her younger siblings and kept a diary filled with the details of her life. The entry for December 25, 1977, recounted all of the gifts she received but concluded with the realization that she "learned how much she loved her mom and dad."

John Shelton said that his daughter was an obedient child at home who always strove to be the best at everything she did. When she recognized a mistake in her computer homework, she insisted on going to school early in order to correct it. She joined the Burger Chef team after a stint at the Dunkin' Donuts franchise next door but had recently turned in her resignation because she felt she'd taken on more than her fair share of responsibility. Store manager Robert Gilyeat liked Ruth Ellen a lot and didn't want to see her go. He asked if she might stay on a few more weeks rather than leave the restaurant short-staffed over the holidays, and she agreed.

When Rachel dropped Ruth Ellen off at the store on Friday afternoon, she paused in the parking lot to admire her little girl, who was growing into a beautiful young woman with her whole life in front of her. *What a great time to be alive*, she thought to herself, putting the car in reverse and pulling away.

Near the back of the store, Mark Flemmonds, sixteen, was cleaning the grill and hanging up his spatulas for the night. The youngest of seven children born to Robert and Blondell Flemmonds, Mark was raised in a devout Jehovah's Witness household. Although Mark had some trouble adjusting to the rigors of high school and struggled throughout his freshman year, he rallied during the first months of the fall semester and was succeeding as a sophomore. Speedway High School officials were convinced that the friendly boy who took pride in his appearance would make it after all. His father was also encouraged by Mark's scholastic improvement and allowed him to take a job at the Burger Chef, which was close enough to home that Mark could walk back and forth to work.

Mark enjoyed his position as a short-order cook and readily agreed to switch shifts when his co-worker, seventeen-year-old Ginger Haggard, needed that Friday night off. However, at the last minute, he tried to renege on his agreement, but Gilyeat told Mark that a deal was a deal and that he would be expected to work.

"I feel really bad about the whole thing," Haggard said.

Daniel returned from the restroom and got to work bagging up the garbage before taking it out to the dumpster. He was a junior at Decatur Central High School who loved to laugh, tell jokes and have a good time. He was relatively new to the Friday night shift, having been moved to the closing crew after Speedway High School senior Diana Dillon left her position the week before.

"Daniel Davis took my place," she said. "There's no question I would have been there. That was my shift."

Daniel had a passion for photography and often developed his pictures at home in his own darkroom. He was also fascinated with aviation and planned to enlist in the U.S. Air Force after high school. Like the other three,

Illustration from a Burger Chef employee hygiene manual that was distributed to crew members in the 1970s. By the time of the murders, the employee uniform had changed in terms of color and design. *Author's private collection.*

he was a model employee who never gave Gilyeat any trouble. In fact, the manager said all three of the students easily worked between twenty and thirty hours each week while maintaining their grades, and they had earned his trust. When he thought about it, he could not remember a time that any of them had been late for their shifts. They were truly an exceptional crew.

"They were kids who were out there trying to take responsibility," Cherne said.

But that night, they were in the wrong place at the wrong time.

Chapter 2

A ROBBERY GONE WRONG?

J ust after midnight on November 18, Brian Kring drove by the Crawfordsville Road Burger Chef on his way home for the night. The seventeen-year-old was an employee of the franchise, but he was not on duty when he pulled into the parking lot and cut his engine. There were no other cars in the parking lot, but he saw that the interior lights were on, indicating that a few of the crew members were still inside the store cleaning. He decided to go in, visit with his friends and help them close the store before heading home to his parents.

Knowing the front doors would be locked, Brian walked to the rear of the building to knock, but to his surprise, he found the door ajar. *That's weird*, he thought, entering the restaurant. He called out a greeting, but no one responded. The place was eerily silent as he made his way through the kitchen to the front counter, where he found the cash register drawers lying empty on the tiled floor. Concerned, he went into the manager's office only to discover that it looked as if it had been ransacked. All of the evidence suggested that the Burger Chef had been robbed, but where were the employees?

Brian's eyes fell onto a jacket that was crumpled on the floor as if its owner had abandoned it. He recognized it immediately as the jacket he remembered seeing Ruth Ellen Shelton wearing on Friday. Why would she leave it behind on such a chilly November night? Fear crept over his body as he reached for the phone in order to dial 911. He told the dispatcher who answered about the open door, the empty cash drawers and the chaos in the manager's office. The person on the other end of the line promised to send someone right away and instructed that he should stay put until they arrived. Brian thanked the operator and hung up, but he couldn't shake the horrible feeling that his co-workers may have been kidnapped.

When the Speedway police arrived, they found few clues. There were two empty currency bags and an empty roll of adhesive tape next to the open safe in the manager's office, but the safe still contained over $100 in rolled coins. Store manager Robert Gilyeat arrived on the scene and tallied the receipts from the evening. He estimated that nearly $600 in cash was missing from the store in addition to the four employees.

With no signs of a forced entry or struggle, the police wondered if the robbery was an inside job. Maybe the crew went to a nearby under-twenty-one club or out for a joyride on the company's dime. It wasn't unheard of for Burger Chef employees to pick up a pizza or donuts to eat as they closed, but to steal money from their employer and go out on the town? That seemed highly unlikely to Gilyeat given the stellar track record of his crew, not to mention the fact that the two girls left their jackets and purses behind. Girls don't usually leave without those items unless they are forced to. Gilyeat

Rear view of a Burger Chef restaurant in Cookville, Tennessee, showing the kind of door Brian Kring would have found ajar when he stopped by the Crawfordsville Road store just after midnight on November 18, 1978. *Courtesy of Kyle Brown's Burger Chef Memories website.*

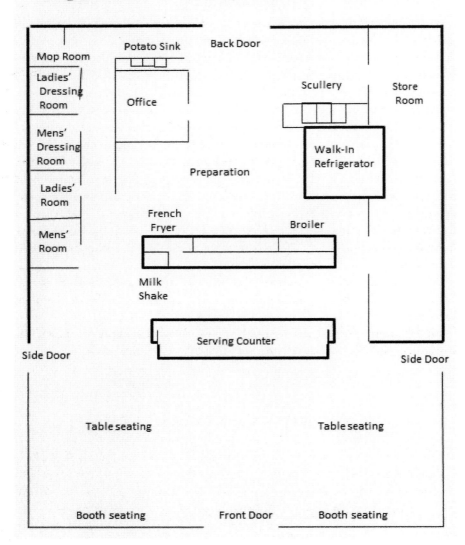

Burger Chef "Cosmopolitan II" Floor Plan

Diagram of a Burger Chef restaurant floor plan after the company switched from the "Open Kite" design to the W-II plan in the 1970s. *Author's own work.*

knew his employees to be a responsible group of kids. They would never rob him or leave the restaurant with the lights blazing and the back door standing open. There had to be another explanation.

Police officers questioned Brian about the open door, and he explained that the door was to remain locked at all times unless one of the crew members was taking the trash to the nearby dumpster. He couldn't be sure of course, but perhaps when one of the employees opened the back door to remove the trash, someone muscled their way in.

It was a definite possibility. Late-night closings and early-morning openings at area fast-food franchises provided plenty of opportunity for armed robbers in the 1970s, and central Indiana was not immune to the phenomenon. On September 26, 1972, a scar-faced bandit armed with a 12-gauge shotgun robbed the Burger Chef franchise at 116th Street and Keystone Avenue just after midnight while the crew was cleaning up for the night. Two men broke in and robbed a far north side McDonald's at gunpoint at 2:00 a.m. on February 6, 1973, and on March 15, 1976, an East Washington Street Steak 'n Shake was robbed of $1,200 when two men entered the rear door at 3:00 a.m. and announced their holdup.

As the night wore on with no sign of the employees, authorities were less likely to think of the incident as a simple prank perpetrated by the teenage employees.

"If I thought it was a kids' prank, I sure would not have stayed up all night working on it," Speedway police lieutenant William Crafton said.

ANOTHER PECULIAR CASE

Crafton's frustration was easy to understand. The disappearance of the four Burger Chef employees was the latest in a long line of bizarre events to plague the town of Speedway in the past few months, and no one in the police department was excited to investigate yet another baffling case.

The first occurred on Saturday, July 29, when sixty-five-year-old Julia Scyphers was shot dead in the garage of her Cunningham Road home. According to Scyphers's husband, Fred, a man with long, dark hair came to the door at approximately 3:00 p.m. asking to see some crystal, china and silver Julia had on display at a recent garage sale. Fred called out to his wife, who assumed the man standing on her porch was the same individual who called about those very items only a few weeks before. He'd made an appointment to come and see them at that time but never showed up. Nonetheless, she still had the items and agreed to open her garage door to let him inspect the merchandise.

A few minutes later, Fred heard a loud noise and went outside to investigate. As he made his way toward the garage, he saw the man get into his white, two-door car, back out of the driveway and speed off. Fred went into the garage to check on his wife and was horrified to find her lying in a pool of her own blood next to their Cadillac. A neighbor called for an ambulance and attempted to resuscitate Julia until help arrived. She was transferred to Wishard Hospital (the former city hospital), where she was pronounced dead a mere forty minutes later.

The shooting was a mystery for investigators. Speedway was a relatively safe community with a low crime rate, so a random act of violence visited upon a middle-class housewife was noteworthy to say the least. As authorities investigated the incident, they concluded that it looked to be a professional hit job, but who would want to kill Julia Scyphers? She was a well-respected member of the community who belonged to the Speedway Christian Church, served as a Girl Scout leader and worked in the Speedway Library. It seemed highly unlikely that she had any enemies who wanted to do her harm.

After ruling out every other motive that was not revenge related, police learned that Julia did have a strained relationship with a local businessman named Brett Kimberlin who employed Julia's daughter Sandra Barton. When Kimberlin became a little too friendly with Barton's teenage daughter, Julia moved the girl into her home to keep her safe and considered filing a peace bond against Kimberlin to prevent him from coming around.

Police were fairly certain that Kimberlin himself was not the person who pulled the trigger; after all, Julia and Fred would have recognized him. But they believed he might be the individual behind the murder contract. Although concrete evidence remained elusive, investigators hoped they might be able to close in on him quickly. However, before they could make an arrest, the Speedway police found themselves embroiled in a new mystery that would rattle the community and turn the Scyphers murder case on its ear.

On September 1, barely a month beyond the death of Julia Scyphers, three explosions rang out, sparking a series of events that would shake Speedway to its core. The first blast occurred around 9:50 p.m. in a trash container at the Speedway Shopping Center at 6000 Crawfordsville Road. The second detonated just after 10:00 p.m. in a dumpster behind the Speedway Motel

THE SPEEDWAY BOMBINGS SEPTEMBER 1978

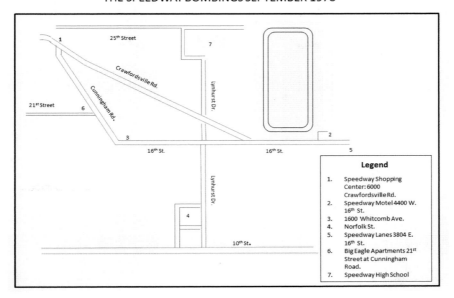

Map of the Speedway bombings, a series of events that occurred one month after the cold-blooded killing of Julia Scyphers during the first week of September 1978; the two incidents were later proved to be related. *Author's own work.*

at 4400 West 16th Street, and the third ignited at 10:45 p.m. in the 1600 block of Whitcomb Avenue. No one was seriously injured in the explosions, and the damage was estimated at less than $10,000. However, the bombings terrorized the town and struck fear in the hearts of its citizens.

"We don't tend to have too many explosions around here, let alone three in one night," Speedway police corporal Gary Donaldson said.

"Something weird was going on in Speedway," said Michael Grider, a 1973 graduate of Speedway High School.

Over the next few days, five similar explosions occurred, including one outside the Speedway Lanes bowling alley, one beneath the squad car of an off-duty police officer and one in the parking lot of Speedway High School, which injured three people. Right from the start, the police believed the same person or group put the bombs in place. They were all cheaply made using a smokeless explosive material that was packed into a soda can and detonated with the same basic timer; shreds of a green plastic trash bag were also found at the various locations, signaling a single bomber, but officially, the police had no suspects.

Unofficially, it was a different story. With every explosion, authorities found more pieces to the puzzle, and it wasn't long before they were able to identify the kind of timer that was used and locate the only store in town that sold it. Investigators spoke to employees and showed them pictures of possible suspects. One employee pointed to a specific man and said he was the person who bought the devices. It was none other than Brett Kimberlin, the same individual who employed Julia Scyphers's daughter and was suspected of being the mastermind behind Julia's murder. (It would be three years before Kimberlin was formally charged with the Speedway bombings or his associate William Bowman was identified as the man who came to the Scypherses' house in July.)

Faced with the disappearance of four fast-food employees, Crafton knew the community could not take another mystery. He needed to find those kids and fast. He had no idea who had taken them or what led to their possible kidnapping, but with every passing moment, he knew he was less likely to find them alive and unharmed.

Telling the Parents

When the Burger Chef crew members failed to return to the restaurant, police began making the phone call every parent dreads receiving. Carolyn Friedt was shocked by the news that her daughter Jayne was missing. She felt security at the Burger Chef had been excellent, especially after the September bombings—one of which detonated across the street from where Jayne worked. Although several crew members quit after the incident, Jayne remained loyal to her job and the employees. Yes, she often worked late hours, but Jayne assured her mother that she felt safe and Speedway police officers regularly stopped by to check on them.

Jayne even told her mother what she would do in the event there was ever a holdup while she was at work. She said she wouldn't fight but rather would give the perpetrator whatever he or she wanted if it meant protecting herself and ensuring the safety of her co-workers.

Jayne's father, George Friedt, was a Conrail train conductor who was in St. Louis at the time of his daughter's disappearance. When he heard the news, he rushed back to Indiana in order to be by his wife's side. He said the news of Jayne's abduction rattled him to his core. "You read about stuff like this happening, but you don't think it can happen to you," he said.

It was 1:00 a.m. when the phone rang at the Shelton residence. Rachel was asleep and didn't hear the call come through, but her husband, John, was awake to answer it. He had no reason to suspect it might be bad news. In fact, he assumed it was Ruth Ellen telling him that she was leaving work and would be home soon. She called every night she was at the Burger Chef, and it was his custom to stay up waiting for the phone to ring so that he could open the garage door for her.

Rachel often wondered how she could sleep so easily while her oldest daughter was working late. After all, mothers are naturally supposed to worry about the safety of their children, but Rachel had a firm belief that if she had done everything in her power, then it was up to God to take care of the rest.

But this time, it wasn't Ruth Ellen on the other end of the line. Instead, it was the Speedway police calling to inform John that his daughter and three others were missing. John gently woke his wife to tell her what had happened. Numbly, she put on a robe and went into the kitchen to await further news, but inside, she felt like she was dying. "I was on the verge of falling apart at the seams and I knew it," Rachel wrote in her diary.

When the police called Robert Flemmonds, they were somewhat vague about what had occurred. For reasons that were never fully explained, they asked if Mark had come home from work yet, and when Robert said he hadn't, the police asked him to call when his son returned. Only later did the elder Flemmonds realize that his son and the others were actually missing. Mark wasn't the kind of kid to stay out late, and when he didn't come home at all, Robert went to the police station in order to find out what had happened.

On the way, he thought back to a moment only a few weeks earlier when he ordered Mark to quit his job at the fast-food place. The boy had become too involved with a female co-worker, and Robert felt the boy didn't need the distraction. The girl quit not long afterward, and Mark persuaded his father to allow him to return to the Burger Chef. In that moment, he wished he hadn't changed his mind.

"I guess…some things, you can't do anything about," he said.

With four sets of parents waiting for news, the Speedway police set out in search of the missing young people. Though they were still unsure as to what had happened to them or if they left the restaurant of their own accord, authorities knew they needed to find them. Reserve and off-duty officers from the Marion County Sheriff's Department joined the hunt as helicopters scanned the region from the air. The Indiana State Police issued an alert on the Burger Chef employees, and the FBI offered to help in any way it could. After a few nervous hours, the police located Jayne's white 1974 Chevrolet Vega at 4:30 a.m. on the 5000 block of West 15th Street, less than two blocks from Speedway Police Headquarters. The driver's side door was locked, but the passenger door was not. The keys were nowhere to be found. Carolyn Friedt said Jayne kept the driver's side door locked at all times, even when she was driving, which suggested that she had been behind the wheel at some point during the night and exited the vehicle via the opposite door.

Crime scene lab specialists searched the car and dusted it for fingerprints, but they failed to find any substantial clues. There was a brown shoe in the car that was similar to a pair found by search parties at the 21st Street bridge near the Eagle Creek, but there was no reason to suspect that the footwear was in any way connected to the crime. The police were merely grasping at whatever straw they thought might be able to help find the missing employees.

Police were disappointed that the discovery of the car yielded few results, but they did not believe Jayne, or the other crew members, abandoned it voluntarily. With the evidence they had at the time, authorities began to formulate a possible narrative as to what might have occurred. Based on

A white 1974 Chevrolet Vega similar to the one Jayne Friedt owned. It was found abandoned on the 5000 block of West 15th Street, less than two blocks from the Speedway police station. *Courtesy of a private collection.*

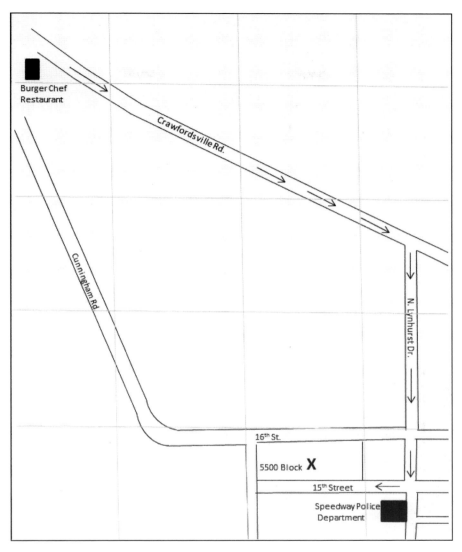

A map showing the location of the Crawfordsville Road Burger Chef and where the police found Jayne Friedt's abandoned car. *Author's own work.*

the information given to them by Brian Kring and the fact that the crew members never returned, police speculated that at some point between 11:00 p.m. Friday and 12:15 a.m. Saturday, one of the crew members—most likely one of the boys—unlocked the back door to take out the trash. He emptied at least one container and was in the process of taking out the rest when something went wrong—very wrong. Someone was outside waiting, and when the door opened, he or she seized the opportunity to break in without a fight.

After robbing the store of its ready cash, the suspect or suspects forced all or part of the kids into Jayne's car and instructed her to drive. Police believed there must have been a second vehicle involved that followed the white Vega east on Crawfordsville Road for seven blocks until it turned south onto Lynhurst Drive. Three blocks later, the vehicles may have turned west onto 15th Street, where the car was ultimately abandoned.

But what happened after that, and more importantly, where were the employees now? Why were they kidnapped in the first place? Were the robbers recognized by one of the employees? With a mysterious motive for taking the teens and no demand for ransom, the only thing the police could do was to keep searching and wait. It was a wait that was particularly agonizing for the parents.

"It just doesn't make any sense," Carolyn Friedt said. "They've got their money and they made an escape. Now why the devil don't they give us back our children?"

Chapter 3

INTO THE WOODS

News of the abductions had yet to hit the media when Burger Chef crew members arrived on Saturday to start their shift. Officers at the scene told them there had been a burglary at the restaurant overnight but little else about what may have occurred. Investigators were still unsure as to what exactly happened in the wee hours of the morning, did not want to speculate about what they did not know and certainly didn't want to publicize the details.

Rather, they permitted the employees to finish cleaning the store so that they could open for business as usual. In the process of readying the restaurant for the lunch rush, every surface was wiped down and the remaining garbage was removed. Unfortunately, so was any evidence that may have existed. In addition, there were no photos taken of the original crime scene, and the store was never dusted for fingerprints. Detectives realized their mistake and returned to the store later in the day to reconstruct the scene from memory, but it was too late. The best chance of finding any forensic evidence had passed. While everyone had the best of intentions, authorities acknowledged that mistakes were made and blunders occurred.

"We screwed it up from the beginning," said retired Speedway police officer Buddy Ellwanger.

John and Rachel's other two children were asleep when the police called the Shelton residence to alert them of Ruth Ellen's disappearance, and the couple didn't have the heart to wake them with the awful news. They decided

The view from behind the counter of a Burger Chef restaurant in Greenbriar (Indianapolis), circa 1970–71. When crew members arrived on the morning of November 18, police allowed them to finish their cleaning procedures, destroying any potential evidence that might remain on the premises. *Courtesy of Kyle Brown's Burger Chef Memories website.*

to wait until morning to tell them that their sister was missing, and as they sat by the phone waiting for the police to call, Rachel reached for her Bible and began to pray for her daughter's safety.

"I found a number of scriptures to stand on. I read a while and I prayed a while....I asked the Lord to put His arms around her. I said, 'God is still in control.'" Rachel wrote in her diary.

Time passed as Rachel sat alone, and at one point, John took her hand and reminded her that Ruth Ellen was their spunky girl who would break away and call home if it were at all possible for her to do so.

But that call never came. By Saturday afternoon, Ruth Ellen and the others were still missing, and the Sheltons knew it was only a matter of time before the newspapers, television and radio stations picked up the story. They knew they had to call family and friends to tell them what had happened before they heard about it on the evening news. Loved ones, shocked by the turn of events, gathered at John and Rachel's home to sit with them and pray for Ruth Ellen's safe return. Saturday night segued into Sunday morning.

"We got very little sleep," Rachel wrote.

None of the families were sleeping very well. As Robert Flemmonds awaited word about his son, he was haunted by a conversation he had with Mark while watching television one night. The program featured a kidnap scene, which prompted Mark to tell his father that if he were ever captured, he'd find a way to escape. He said he would break away, bobbing and weaving as he ran in order to be a harder target to hit.

"I wouldn't lay still and die," Mark said.

It was the kind of statement that gave Robert hope that he would see his child again and buoyed his spirits when he was tired. However, if the families of the four crew members were exhausted by then, so, too, were the officers searching high and low for the kids. The case was their top priority, and as the first reports of the kidnapping appeared in the *Indianapolis News* and on WIBC 1070, authorities encouraged anyone with information pertaining to the incident to come forward. It was a plea that would garner their first solid lead in the case.

TWO MEN IN A PARKING LOT

An hour before Brian Kring pulled into the Burger Chef parking lot and discovered the back door open, another teen was on the premises. It was a sixteen-year-old west side youth who had picked up his girlfriend after her shift at a nearby business and was planning to walk her home. After cutting through the parking lot of the still brightly lit restaurant, the two stole behind the building for a private moment alone.

According to the teens, sometime between 11:15 and 11:30 p.m., two men approached the couple as they sat beside the railroad tracks. Both were white, looked to be in their early to mid-thirties and were dressed in shabby clothes. One of the men, who had dark hair along with a full beard and mustache, asked the boy to identify himself. He held a handkerchief close to his face when he spoke as if he were wiping his nose at the same time. The other man, who was clean-shaven and sported lighter hair, said nothing.

After explaining that they were merely talking, the bearded man told the young man to take his girlfriend home. He implied that it wasn't safe to be loitering about because there had been a lot of vandalism in the area. The kids heeded the advice and left, once again cutting through the Burger Chef parking lot and passing a white Vega along the way.

The pair didn't think anything about the exchange at the time, but after hearing about the disappearance of the Burger Chef crew Saturday afternoon, they wondered if they should tell the police what had occurred. It didn't seem like much, but maybe it would help. They contacted the Speedway Police Department, which was very interested in what the couple had to say. The authorities asked the kids to come in for an interview, and when the couple arrived, investigators talked to them for over an hour about their conversation with the men. Investigators even brought in a hypnotist to help them remember specific details about that night and promised that their identities would be protected. Four decades later, the identities of the teenage couple have never been released.

The teenagers weren't the only ones who saw something suspicious on Friday night. A young woman left her boyfriend's apartment near Crawfordsville Road and drove by the Burger Chef restaurant around midnight. She was heading to her home in Johnson County, which was a forty-five-minute drive, and although she did not see any suspicious activity, she found it odd that the fast-food place appeared to be open.

I thought they closed earlier than that, she remarked to herself as she passed the restaurant.

Michael Grider was stopped at a red light at 16th Street and Lynhurst when he saw a bearded man in a small car with all of the windows fogged. *Why would those windows be so fogged up like that?* he wondered.

While there is no evidence to suggest that he saw the getaway car, Grider called the police to tell them what he noticed. He was interviewed and hypnotized by the authorities but never found out if his information was helpful to the investigation.

Residents on Lupine Drive told police that they saw both a car and a two-tone van speeding through the neighborhood without their lights on. It was the same street that the Shelton family lived on, but John said he didn't see or hear anything out of the ordinary. One of the residents said she heard a scream as the vehicles passed and noted that the car appeared to be full of kids. The car and van made an abrupt stop, and she saw someone get out of the van and walk over to the car. Others said the vehicles slowed to a crawl as they traveled down the 3000 block of Lupine, but they weren't sure if either actually stopped.

A Grisly Discovery

Authorities continued the search for the missing Burger Chef employees on Sunday morning, but with so little to go on and no call from the captors demanding a ransom in return for the crew's safe return, they felt as if they were spinning their wheels. They had no positive identification of the two men who were seen in the restaurant's parking lot on Friday night, and they still had no idea where the four young people had been taken after abandoning Jayne Friedt's Vega early Saturday morning.

That afternoon, there was finally a break when the Indiana State Police received a call from Johnson County resident Fred Heger, who owned a heavily wooded property at Stones Crossing Road—a half mile east of State Road 37. At approximately 3:15 p.m., Fred and his wife, Rosemary, went for an afternoon walk, and as they ambled along in the crisp autumn air, they happened upon a grisly discovery: the bodies of Ruth Ellen Shelton and Daniel Davis lying facedown in the dirt. Fred immediately recognized the fast-food uniform Ruth Ellen was wearing and realized that they must be two of the missing Burger Chef employees. Several yards away, he located the bodies of Mark Flemmonds and Jayne Friedt as well.

Shaken, the Hegers returned home to alert the authorities about their find. Within minutes, officers and detectives from a number of agencies descended on the property to investigate. Indiana State Police lieutenant Jim Cramer was among the troopers who were called to help early on, and despite his considerable experience, he found the crime scene disturbing.

"I'd seen people shot before, but I guess that was the most upsetting. You're talking about four young people who, by all appearances, had done nothing to cause their own death," he said.

WIBC's Lee Daniels hovered above from a helicopter and noted that from the sky, the Hegers' property was an innocent-looking wooded area. "There's a corn field bordering it on the east, several houses stand at the west. A small stream runs in the northeast corner. Power lines that stretch over the top. There's really no evidence that any violence ever took place in this wooded area except on the lane that runs up the west side there are parked at least four Indiana State Police units and Johnson County units. They are guarding what is a very macabre murder scene."

The bodies were found in a small glen at the center of the woods in an area measuring approximately three hundred feet in diameter. Daniel and Ruth Ellen were lying side by side while Mark and Jayne were found lying in opposite directions, forming something of a triangle shape. None of the employees was bound in any way, and there was nothing on their clothing to suggest a struggle.

Confident that they had found the missing Burger Chef employees, authorities secured what they believed to be the crime scene and began to sweep the area for evidence. Like the scene at the restaurant, there was little to be found, which frustrated those in search of clues. There was no vehicle in the vicinity, but there was a tire track on the driveway that police made a plaster mold of in hopes that they could identify a possible make and model. Investigators were also studying a .38-caliber revolver that was found in Speedway near 21st Street and Cunningham Drive. They did not know if it could be connected to the murders, but if it was, then perhaps it might shed some light on the route taken by the killer or killers in order to reach the Heger property.

Officers questioned Fred and Rosemary about anything they might have seen or heard over the weekend, but the couple had no idea when or how the bodies might have ended up in their woods. The property included a curved private drive that wound around a hill overlooking the rest of the land, but they had not seen any vehicles, heard the crunch of the gravel or noticed anything out of the ordinary over the course of the weekend. It was clear that the discovery of the bodies on their land upset the Hegers considerably, and the police were quick to assure them that they would do all they could to protect their anonymity where the public was concerned. Unfortunately, not every press outlet adhered to that promise, and several released the couple's name in subsequent reports.

At 4:45 p.m., Johnson County coroner Richard Tudor arrived and pronounced the four young people dead at the scene. He arranged for the bodies to be transported to Johnson County Memorial Hospital in Franklin and for former coroner Dr. Harley Palmer to conduct autopsies on the crew members. He told reporters present that he hoped to announce the results of the postmortems in a day or two, but until he knew more, he refused to speculate on the cause/causes of death or the number of wounds each crew member sustained.

KINKS IN THE CHAIN OF COMMAND

Although the various entities involved in the early stages of the Burger Chef murders intended to work together in a cooperative effort, turf wars ensued as each agency jockeyed for position and began to work the case in its own way. Naturally, the Speedway police took the lead at the restaurant, but in Johnson County, the chain of command was less clear. Technically, the case fell under the jurisdiction of the Johnson County Sheriff's Department, but because Fred Heger called the Indiana State Police first, they took control of the recovery site. Subsequently, when a sheriff's deputy approached the Heger property in an attempt to help, he was denied access and summarily dismissed.

Johnson County sheriff Tom Pritchard was out of town until Sunday afternoon, but when he returned, he pledged not only his deputy but also two sergeants to assist in any way that they could. Prichard was thanked for his generous offer, but the state police never took him up on it.

Prichard was disappointed. He wasn't trying to usurp the case for his own team; he merely felt that two heads might be better than one. He also felt that his officers would be valuable assets to the investigation because they were more familiar with the area, and he was bothered by the professional slight.

"Other than crime lab equipment," he said, "I felt our department is just as capable [of aiding in the investigation]....If they [the state police] are going to treat us this way, we're not going to bend over backward to help them."

A state police spokesperson refuted the claim and tried to assure the sheriff's department that its assistance was welcome. While he understood the deputies' feelings when they were blocked from meetings at the case command post, the exclusion was not intentional. The added security was merely to ensure that neither members of the public nor of the media had access to their discussions. The issue of exclusion was one that would come up time and again.

Doran Miller was a deputy sheriff in Johnson County at the time and knew how his colleagues felt about the snub, but he tried to keep it in perspective. "Let's be fair to the state police," he said in hindsight. "The more people you get muddling makes the case more difficult."

As it was, the state police had no shortage of company as they combed the woods. As the various departments converged on the site, some drove through areas that should have been sealed off. There were rumors that one of the bodies was moved before the coroner or evidence technician arrived at the scene, and in an effort to positively identify the bodies, state police detective Richard Bumps removed two pieces of identification from one of the victims, put them in the pocket of his overcoat and inadvertently took them home. As if the errors at the restaurant weren't enough, now authorities had two crime scenes that had been compromised.

"That investigation could be used as an example of what not to do," said retired state police investigator Brook Appleby in 1988. "There were mistakes made by all departments involved."

THEY ARE ALL DECEASED

One of those mistakes occurred at 6:00 p.m. when a lieutenant in the homicide branch of the Indianapolis Police Department headquarters rushed out of his office and announced to the desk sergeant, "They found those kids!" He was unaware that Patrick Morrison, a reporter for the *Indianapolis Star* who had been assigned to cover the story, was sitting nearby. He'd been camped out at the police station over the weekend awaiting any word in the fate of the four Burger Chef employees. When Morrison's head snapped to attention at the leak, the lieutenant realized he'd spoken out of turn and quickly rounded on the journalist.

"You didn't hear that," he warned.

There was a very good reason for keeping the news private for the time being. The families of the four victims were still under the impression that their children were merely missing. While the authorities at the murder scene continued the painstaking process of collecting anything that could help them crack the case, the parents were contacted and asked to come into the Speedway police station. One by one, the parents arrived, hoping to be reunited with their children. When everyone was assembled, they were ushered into a small room and told the terrible news. All four of the crew members had been found. They were all deceased.

Rachel Shelton bit into the tissue she was holding while the other parents reacted to the pronouncement in their own unique ways. Each one of them held out hope until the last minute, but now all hope was gone. Tears flowed as the families filed out of the police station, everyone taking the time to embrace one another before heading home to be alone with their grief. The Sheltons' two other children, twelve-year-old Theresa and fifteen-year-old Gordon, were waiting in the kitchen when they heard their parents' car pull into the driveway. They hoped that their sister would be with them and that the nightmare would be over, but when she wasn't there, Rachel tried to deliver the blow as gently as possible.

"Ruth Ellen is in heaven with Jesus," she said sadly.

"She was my only sister," Theresa said in 2013. "I idolized her. I wanted to be as happy and go-lucky as she was. I would have liked to raise our children together. She was a good person."

Having told the families, the Speedway police called a press conference at 10:30 p.m. Sunday night to tell the media that the bodies of the four missing Burger Chef employees had been found, but they provided few additional details at the time. It was believed that an undisclosed weapon was used to shoot all four, but police refused to say how many wounds were inflicted. At least two of the kids had been shot at close range, but it was not clear whether they had been brought into the woods and killed, murdered elsewhere and then brought to the woods or if they were gunned down while trying to make a run for it. Until the autopsies were completed, there were just too many unknowns.

Police would not say whether the kids were found wearing their work uniforms, though most speculated that they were. True to their word, authorities opted not to disclose the name of the Johnson County property owner who discovered the missing crew members, and they refused to confirm or deny the existence of composite drawings depicting the two men who had been seen in the Burger Chef parking lot on the night of the abduction.

"I don't have any answers," state police captain Robert Allen said. "In my mind, it was probably more than one man [who killed the youths]."

Darkness came before investigators could finish gathering evidence, and they made plans to return with metal detectors the following day in hopes of finding any clue that might help solve the mystery. A state police car and various troopers staved off the curious reporters and onlookers who stationed themselves along the front of the property hoping to learn more. When the crowds dispersed, they allowed the Myers Ambulance Service to remove the bodies in order to transport them to the hospital for the postmortem examinations.

Mark Myers was a sixteen-year-old high school student who worked part time for his father, Larry, and had been going on ambulance runs ever since he was a child. He said northwest Johnson County was cold that evening as they made their way to the woods where victims of the quadruple homicide were waiting. Mark was no stranger to traumatic cases, but the Burger Chef case had an entirely different feel to it. The full moon shone through the branches of the bare trees, casting an eerie light on the crew members' remains. As the pair loaded the bodies into the ambulance, Mark said he felt a certain kinship to the deceased kids.

"They were all my age," he said. "I'll never forget that."

Chapter 4

FRONT-PAGE NEWS

On Monday, November 20, newspaper headlines blared the awful news: the bodies of the four young crew members who had been abducted from a Speedway Burger Chef were found in a wooded area of Johnson County. It was the lead story in that morning's edition of the *Indianapolis Star*, just above an article announcing the deaths of five U.S. citizens, including California congressman Leo J. Ryan, in a jungle ambush near Guyana, South America.

At first glance, the two stories could not be further apart, but those who read past the first few lines were horrified to discover the geographic connection between them. It was believed that the November 18 attack was carried out by members of the People's Temple, a religious cult led by Lynn, Indiana native Jim Jones. The group got its start on the near eastside of Indianapolis before moving to California and eventually to the Jonestown compound in Guyana. Later that day, it was reported that 917 members of the religious organization died in an act of mass suicide after drinking a cyanide-laced grape drink. Jones did not take his own life with the others by drinking the poison but rather died of a self-inflicted gunshot to his head.

It was certainly a day for Indiana-related news, and while the Jonestown mass suicide was the kind of story that dominated the national conscience, the Burger Chef murders weighed heavily in the hearts and minds of those in central Indiana—especially Speedway residents who had been through so much in the past few months. They were shocked, sickened and angry about the latest event to hit their community, and some no longer felt safe in their own homes. Others said they didn't want to let their children out of their sight. Many felt that that the Speedway Police Department was doing little to protect the public and had no confidence in the agency's ability to solve any of the recent crimes.

"It's so useless," a female resident said to a WIBC reporter. "I didn't know them [the Burger Chef victims] personally, but I am just heartbroken about it because I have kids that age."

The woman said although she always loved living in Speedway and often went shopping at night because the stores were less crowded, it was a practice she didn't plan to continue.

"All of a sudden last night was the first time I thought 'I won't do it again.' All of a sudden, I'm afraid and I never have been in this town," she said.

A male resident also expressed his disgust at what he called "stupid, ignorant type of killings that never should have happened" and were probably carried out by someone who was sick in the mind.

"I manage a restaurant myself and I've noticed what's happening out here in Speedway with the bombings and now the killings and I have taken measures where I am armed when I am not in my business," he said.

The police officers understood the community's reaction to the murders, and no one wanted to see the case resolved more than them, but that was not going to be easy when authorities could not identify a specific motive and had so little evidence to go on. Why would anyone kill four people over $581? It didn't make any sense. If the perpetrators were motivated by money alone, why were the girls' purses left behind at the restaurant along with hundreds of dollars in change? Cash was found in the front pocket of Jayne Friedt's striped uniform shirt when her body was discovered, and one of the other victims was wearing a watch that could have been pawned for a few bucks. Why didn't the killers take either?

There were additional questions nagging investigators as well. Why were the crew members taken to Johnson County, and how did they get there? In addition to dusting Jayne's Vega for fingerprints and examining it for other clues, police were searching a 1973 green Mercury that was found on Sunday night on the 2400 block of Carrolton Avenue. The vehicle was reported stolen on Friday night from an area near the Burger Chef, but officers did not know if the car might have been involved in the abduction.

Were Jayne and the others forced to leave the restaurant and drive to another spot before being packed into a van, station wagon or other vehicle and driven to Johnson County? Was more than one vehicle involved? Did they drive past the Scyphers residence on Cunningham and lose a weapon on the way back to Crawfordsville Road before hopping on I-465 and State Road 37 in order to arrive at their final destination? Were the killers familiar with the area? The commute would have taken only thirty or forty minutes, putting them at the Heger property well before 6:00 a.m. on Saturday. Authorities speculated that the kids could have been killed as early as 3:00 a.m. However, their bodies were not found until the following day. Were there other stops along the way? Were they held hostage for a period of time?

Johnson County prosecutor D. Charles Gantz wasn't sure, and he didn't know why the secluded lane in White River Township was chosen for the crime. "At this time, we can't rule out the possibility that somebody local was involved," he said.

"Whoever did this didn't expect these bodies to be found for several months, if ever," said another Indiana State Police investigator.

Officers spoke to neighbors of the Hegers and chased down every piece of information they could get their hands on, but nothing substantial was reported. One neighbor said she heard gunshots around the alleged time of the murder, but her husband assured her that the noise came from a television show he was watching at the time. Another neighbor heard dogs barking that night, and yet another said they saw flashlights and heard screams coming from the Heger property, but none of the statements led to any concrete evidence.

Like those living in Speedway, residents of rural Johnson County were rattled by the horrific crime. Cheryl Gerdt, who lived across from the wooded area where the bodies were found, said she was frightened by the events of the weekend and was hesitant to let her two children play in the area for fear that the killer or killers were familiar with the location and may still be out there somewhere.

"To come all the way from Speedway to here, they would have to have known something about the area, unless [while driving south] it was the first isolated area they came to," she said.

In addition to speaking with folks near the Heger property, officers were keen to talk to anyone who may have been in or near the Burger Chef restaurant on the night of November 17, and they followed up on any credible lead that came into the command post, including an assertion by one individual who said they remembered seeing Jayne in a car on Crawfordsville Road in the early hours of November 18. However, none of the tips could help them piece together what happened that ended with the murders of four young people.

Frustrated, investigators decided to cast a wider net. They expanded their search beyond the primary and secondary locations. They looked into any seemingly similar event throughout the state and around the country in hopes of finding a connection. Was it possible that the Burger Chef murders may be part of something bigger?

THE PLOT THICKENS

One case in Oklahoma City, Oklahoma, looked especially promising. Earlier in the year on July 16, five employees of the Sirloin Stockade were found shot to death in a refrigeration unit of the restaurant. A sixth victim still fluttered with life and was transported to the hospital, but she, too, died before being able to give authorities more information as to what had happened. Two of the victims were middle-aged men, but the other four were all under the age of eighteen. At the time, detectives had no suspects, but it was later determined that the crime was committed by Roger Dale Stafford; his wife, Verna; and his brother Harold. Less than a month before, they had shot a North Dakota family by pretending to be stranded interstate travelers.

A Sirloin Stockade restaurant sign in Hobbs, New Mexico. On July 16, 1978, five employees of a similar restaurant in Oklahoma were found shot to death in the refrigeration unit of the establishment. *John Margolies Roadside America Collection for the Library of Congress.*

There was another case in October in which a pregnant woman working by herself in a Milwaukee food store was found shot to death in a park several miles away. Detectives also looked into a rash of fast-food store robberies, but no direct connection could be found. Refusing to give up hope, police set up a special hotline to collect tips in hope that someone would say something that would connect all the dots and lead to the killers. They encouraged anyone with any information to call the number.

"They might think something is minute, but it could be very important to us," Lieutenant William Crafton said.

After Burger Chef manager Robert Gilyeat officially identified his deceased employees in the morgue and Dr. Harley Palmer completed the autopsies, Palmer filled out the necessary paperwork and released the bodies on Monday night to the families for burial. The Hall-Baker Funeral Home in Plainfield collected Jayne's body, while Ruth Ellen Shelton's was transported to the Flanner and Buchannan Speedway Chapel. Daniel Davis's body was taken to the Farley Mann Road Chapel, and Mark Flemmonds's remains were prepared at the Williams Funeral Home in Indianapolis.

Though Palmer was keen to keep the details of his examinations under wraps as much as possible, in case his information could compromise the investigation, his postmortems showed that Ruth Ellen and Daniel had been shot multiple times in the head, neck and shoulders as they lay on the ground next to each other. Jayne was stabbed twice in the heart with a five-inch hunting knife, the blade of which was protruding from her chest when her body was discovered. Mark died after receiving a blow to the head, which may or may not have occurred as a result of a beating. Palmer confirmed previous reports that there had been no obvious signs of a struggle on the kids' work uniforms and few clues on their remains. Although it was impossible to determine the exact time of death, Palmer believed that the employees were killed quickly upon their arrival in the woods and not held hostage for an extended period.

While authorities maintained that the bodies of the four crew members were found in a triangular pattern, they were not convinced that the kids started out that way. Investigators speculated that all four were probably lying on the ground when the murders began, but when the first shots were fired at Ruth Ellen and Daniel, the other two possibly jumped up and ran in opposite directions in an effort to flee. It made sense. After all, because none of them was restrained in any way, it may have been their best chance at an escape. Unfortunately, Jayne's chance of survival was short-lived when she was recaptured and subsequently stabbed, but Mark's death was puzzling. Was it possible that under the cloak of darkness, the sophomore managed to evade his killers only to run headlong into a tree and die? His autopsy suggested that he sustained some kind of internal injury and had choked on his own blood, so there were still too many unknowns about what had occurred.

The fact that the four Burger Chef employees were killed in three distinct ways was particularly significant to detectives and gave credence to the probability that there was more than one suspect involved. However, who they might have been and why they would kill four individuals for $581 was a mystery that still didn't add up unless something went wrong somewhere along the way. One of the investigators wondered if the perpetrators actually planned on killing anyone at all. Perhaps the suspects cased the restaurant on Thursday night only to run into trouble when they returned to rob the place the following evening. It was an interesting theory, but what could have been different about Friday?

The only thing that stood out in Gilyeat's mind was the fact that Mark was on the schedule. He was not in the habit of working on Friday nights, but he had agreed to switch shifts with a co-worker. Was his presence the component that thwarted the caper? It was an idea at least one detective was willing to entertain.

"They may have been surprised when Mark Flemmonds was on duty," he said, under the condition of anonymity. "He could have recognized them— called them by name—and the bandits, who were now identified, decided to kill all of the employees."

Another factor that also put Mark as the catalyst for the killing was the fact that his body was found 160 feet away from the other three. Was he led away from the others to be beaten only to die as a result of his injuries? When he died, were the killers compelled to silence the rest of the employees? It was fair speculation, but most of the investigators remained tight-lipped about the crime and were careful not to let too many of the details slip. There had been so much publicity surrounding the Scyphers murder and the Speedway bombings that they didn't want to do anything that could compromise their investigation.

Unfortunately, the investigation was already compromised, and the window of opportunity to make up for lost ground was closing fast. Crime scene investigators know that the first forty-eight hours are critical if they hope to solve a particular mystery, but in this case, the first forty-eight hours were more than a little messy, and they couldn't make up for the errors that occurred early on. They had to do their best not to make another mistake.

Johnson County coroner Dick Tudor was unwilling to speculate on even the smallest detail because he felt the facts could be organized much more thoroughly when only a few people had access to all of them.

"If few people have the true facts, it's easier to sort the true from the false [reports]," he said. "What we want to do is to catch the people who did this."

THE PUBLIC'S RIGHT TO KNOW

The lack of information was infuriating to the journalists who were trying to cover the story and eager for any additional details. All detectives would tell them was to focus their attention on the deaths of Jayne and Mark because it was believed the circumstances surrounding those two deaths were vital to the investigation, but they wouldn't say why.

The news embargo was not limited to the media but also included the victims' families and other law enforcement officers who were actively working on the case. Rachel Shelton said once the officers got all of the information out of her that they could regarding her daughter, they no longer called or bothered to update her on the status of the investigation. A Speedway patrolman told *Indianapolis Star* reporters that Lieutenant William Crafton was acting so secretive about the murders that he wasn't even sharing information with them. "How does he expect us to look for anything if we don't know what we are looking for?"

The perceived lack of transparency outraged members of the Hoosier State Press Association (HSPA), who took investigators to task for withholding information about the case. Richard Cardwell, general counsel for the HSPA, asserted that authorities needed the cooperation of the community in order to solve crimes, and Johnson County prosecutor D. Charles Gantz agreed there should be no censorship regarding the case. He felt that the only information that should be withheld was information only the killer or killers would know.

"The number of stab wounds suffered by one of the victims is not that important to the general public, but it is something known to the killer. How the one young man died of head injuries is something we don't know, but the killer does. He may have been struck with a hard object, run into a tree, but frankly we don't know," Gantz said.

In an effort to demonstrate to the public that they were not being deliberately kept out of the loop, the police decided to release the composite sketches of the two men who were seen behind the Burger Chef on the night of November 17. Authorities said that the men were "people of interest" who were wanted for questioning, but they stopped short of labeling the pair suspects. The composites were created from the memories of the teenage eyewitnesses whom the men engaged that Friday night and who were willing to undergo hypnosis in order to remember as many details as they could.

Virgil Vandagriff, a sergeant with the Marion County Sheriff's Department, was brought in to conduct the hypnosis session. Although it was still a new practice and not one that every agency was willing to embrace, Vandagriff was drawn to the technique thanks to his father's interest in the field and was fascinated by its practical application in law enforcement.

Vandagriff spent approximately three hours with the young couple trying to extract as much information from their subconscious as possible. He had the teens fix their gaze on an object in the room and relax their minds and bodies and then gently asked probing questions about the men they encountered. He said a person often registers information in their brain that they cannot bring to a conscious level out of fear, tension or simply trying too hard to remember every detail.

"Hypnosis creates a state of mind in where you can pull that information to the surface," he said.

Prior to being hypnotized, the couple disagreed a bit on their description of the two men, which was frustrating to the sheriff's artist, Lieutenant William Mahler, who wanted to draw as complete a picture as he could. But once they were put under hypnosis by Vandagriff, their accounts were virtually identical. The first man was roughly thirty to forty years old; stood five feet seven or eight inches tall; had a medium build; weighed between 150 and 160 pounds; sported greasy, medium brown hair; was clean-shaven; and at the time was wearing a dark blue jacket with a sheepskin lining along with a pair of blue jeans. The other man, the one who briefly spoke to the couple, appeared to be the same age as his counterpart but had a stockier build. He stood anywhere from five feet six to ten inches tall, weighed approximately 200 pounds and had a reddish-brown beard and mustache. He also wore dark clothing along with a pair of work boots.

"I have no way of knowing if the men in the sketches were involved in the murders, but I am certain that they were the men who were in the parking lot that night," Vandagriff said.

Authorities also disclosed that they had retrieved the .38-caliber slugs that were used to kill Ruth Ellen and Daniel, but they could not connect the bullets with the weapon they had located over the weekend. While it was possible that the ammunition came from a .38-caliber revolver, the bullets could have come from a .357 Magnum or a 9mm pistol as well. They announced that the blade used to kill Jayne contained no fingerprints, but it was unclear if the suspect may have been wearing gloves, if the handle of the knife was broken off during the attack or if it was recovered at the crime scene.

In an effort to further incentivize the public to come forward with any tips, the Burger Chef corporation offered a $25,000 reward for information leading to the arrest and conviction of anyone connected to the murders. Steak 'n Shake, another local restaurant chain, added another $1,000 to the reward money, and memorial funds were established by Burger Chef Systems, as well as the Indiana Restaurant Association. There were rumors that Burger Chef was coerced into offering reward money in addition to the memorial fund for the victims' families, but public relations officials were quick to set the record straight: the Speedway Police Department had received numerous calls from members of the public offering up donations, and with no way of establishing and administrating such a collection, Burger Chef offered to manage the funds for them.

Naturally, the promise of a monetary reward caused a flood of calls to the Speedway police station from any number of individuals claiming to recognize the suspects. Less than a week after the abduction, an unidentified bearded man was questioned for more than an hour at the Speedway police station but was later released. State police and Speedway police officers converged on the Big Eagle Apartments not long after a visit from one of the victims' family members suggested a tip, but nothing came of that lead either.

Within twenty-four hours of publishing the special hotline number, one hundred calls had been received. Although the police knew that the majority of them would be false leads, they hoped among the numerous tips someone would offer up a nugget of information that could lead to a major break.

"In this case," a spokesperson for the Indiana State Police said, "we've got to hope that the killer or killers may have told someone who has a conscience who will come forward."

Chapter 5

SYMPATHY AND SUPPORT

W hile law enforcement agencies squabbled, speculated and faced setbacks in the early days of the investigation, the families of the victims had the unenviable task of making funeral and burial arrangements for their children who had been taken from them in a brutal act of violence. Memorial services for Daniel Davis, Jayne Friedt and Ruth Ellen Shelton were scheduled for Wednesday, November 22, with Mark Flemmonds's funeral to follow on November 24, the day after Thanksgiving.

The Speedway Burger Chef paid tribute to the slain employees by dousing the lights of the bonneted "happy face" sign that hailed customers traveling along Crawfordsville Road. They also hung green-and-white memorial wreaths on the restaurant doors along with a sign announcing that the store would remain closed in memory of the crew members until all the funerals were concluded.

That didn't stop the inquisitive from cruising the parking lot, stopping long enough to read the notice before heading around back to see where the killers entered the restaurant and abducted the employees. There was nothing remarkable about the heavy metal door bearing a plaque that read: "No Deliveries Accepted Between 11 A.M. and 1 P.M.," but after the events of the weekend, it was suddenly a roadside curiosity.

The outpouring of sympathy and support from the community was unprecedented. Not only did those who knew the four young people show up in droves to pay their respects, but members of the public also came

A Burger Chef restaurant building in the same style as the Crawfordsville Road store, including the "Happy Bonnet Face" signage that heralded customers from the road. *Courtesy of Scott R. Sanders.*

forward hoping to add to the $25,000 reward offered by the Burger Chef corporation for information leading to the arrest of those responsible for the crime. Burger Chef manager of public relations Rick Bollinger was touched by the community's generosity, but he turned down additional contributions. He suggested that those who wanted to make donations should do so through the memorial fund that the company set up to benefit the victims' families.

"Speedway Police and the Indiana State Police told us that a $25,000 reward should be sufficient," he said.

SAYING GOODBYE

The pastors who were planning eulogies said the services were hard to prepare for and would be even harder to deliver when the time came. While trying to find the right words to comfort the family and friends of the fallen, Reverend Russell F. Blowers of the 91st Street Christian Church said that he chose scriptures that stressed death was not the end of human life. He'd spent a lot of time with Daniel's family over the past few days, and he hoped to incorporate some of the things that had impressed him during that time.

Blowers was especially moved by members of the Decatur Central High School student council who went to every room of the school in order to take up a collection for Daniel's parents. They brought the funds over to the family's home. After considering what to do with the money, Daniel's parents, knowing of their son's passion for photography as a hobby, created a photography scholarship in his honor.

"That impressed me almost more than anything," Blowers said.

It impressed Anthony Etienne as well. As principal of the large high school, he said that those students who knew Daniel liked him a lot. "Different ones have come up to me and wanted to help the family," he said. "Students yesterday were all day long very quiet, there was some discussion about it [the killing]. For those students working evening hours, there was some kind of fear because it is so close to home and they think of those situations. I think that sums up pretty much the mood of the students."

Etienne said he didn't know Daniel well but met him when Daniel came into his office to get a work permit to join the Burger Chef team.

"I asked him why he was so concerned about getting it and he said he was worried about getting the work permit to Burger Chef on time," he recalled.

Blowers paid tribute to all four victims during the service for Daniel on Wednesday. Addressing the 250 people in attendance, he said it was difficult to lead prayers at a funeral where a person's death was the result of

The grave of Daniel Davis at Mount Zion Cemetery in Sullivan, Indiana. *Author's private collection.*

something so senseless and served no larger purpose. He acknowledged that there were three other ministers in the community who would stand beside the bodies of the three other children and attempt to bring words of comfort to the grieving.

"They will have no magic words, no quick answers," he commented.

Teenagers who were still bewildered by the events of the past week turned out wearing everything from blue jeans and cheerleading uniforms to Sunday dresses and stiff sport coats to say goodbye to their friend. As the service began, they tried to remain composed, but as the finality of Daniel's death became a reality, the kids let their tears fall freely. A few were so overcome by emotion that they had to be escorted from the service.

Bruce Roaden, who was a neighbor of Daniel's, described the slain teen as his best friend. He had last seen Daniel in a Friday morning English class at Decatur Central High School the day before the teen died. "We spent a lot of time together talking and laughing and going to movies together—I sure do miss him," he said.

Blowers told the congregation that the executioners of the four precious lives were somewhere in the city, state or country, and he was confident that they would be captured. It was only a matter of time before the public would find out who they were. "Sooner or later they will be caught and judged. The entire city has suffered the tragedy with the family of the victims of the senseless killings,"

Nearly three hundred people packed the Flanner and Buchanan Mortuary in Speedway to say a final farewell to Ruth, the pretty seventeen-year-old with shoulder-length hair and an optimistic smile. She was remembered as a young lady of tremendous faith who had a deep love for her family and enjoyed making crafts for others. In fact, many of her creations were on display as a tribute to her artistic talent. At the time of her death, Ruth was hand-painting a white cloth wrap for the holidays featuring candy canes, Santa Claus and other holiday symbols. A friend eventually finished the piece and presented it to Ruth's parents as a memento of their daughter.

Reverend Jack McCormick stressed the certainty of God for those who were committed to him. He noted Ruth Ellen's participation in his church's youth activities, as well as her commitment to Christ.

"If there was one thing Ruth Ellen would want people to know, [it was] that she was a born-again Christian and that Christ was first in her life," he said.

The Westside Church of the Nazarene Youth Chorale, a group to which Ruth belonged, sang "Safe in the Heart of Jesus" for their friend, and at

The grave of Ruth Ellen Shelton at Washington Park West in Indianapolis. *Author's private collection.*

the end of their performance, they filed by the casket and placed white carnations inside it. As part of Ruth's final outfit, she wore a new gold belt, which her mother intended to give her for Christmas that year. Rachel kept the accessory along with a pair of Ruth's glasses, her old baby shoes and the dress she wore in their final family portrait.

"The night before the funeral…so many teenagers came in with tears in their eyes. I could only tell them to meet her in Heaven," Rachel chronicled in her diary. "The day before Thanksgiving we laid her body to rest. Most of the relatives left. It was all over. But the adjustment was just the beginning."

Although minister William Hendricks at the Avon Christian Church had been a preacher for only four years and was no stranger to presiding over funeral services, he said Jayne's was the hardest he'd ever done. The major difference, in his opinion, was that in most cases, funerals were a fitting end to a full life. "For Jayne, it was just the opposite because she had a lot of potential she never got to share," he said.

On Thursday night, Robert Flemmonds spoke in carefully measured tones about his son Mark. He said from the moment he learned about the kidnapping on Saturday morning, he tried to remain pragmatic about the outcome. Deep down, he knew it would end badly because only a heartless person would abduct four young people who were simply trying to do their jobs. Still, he refrained from responding with bitterness toward those responsible for his son's death. Instead, he offered a message of hope and love to those who committed what he called a "bad act of ignorance."

"Don't get me wrong, I want to see justice because that is the law under which we all must live, but we are a family of repentance. We wouldn't lift a hand against the people who did this. It's possible I will see Mark's killers in Heaven," he said.

Edward Smooth, an elder at the Eagle Creek Congregation of Jehovah's Witness, presided over Mark's service. He was a longtime spiritual advisor to the sophomore and knew him well. He reminded those assembled that everyone came from dust and it was to dust that they would all return. Robert took comfort in the words and said he was confident that his son was praying the entire time he was in the custody of his captors and that he was in God's grace when he passed.

"He was so young—but we know he was straight with his Maker. Mark told us it was his hope to be in God's favor whenever he died and we're happy to know that," Robert said.

Speedway High School principal John Bainbridge said the student council met after school earlier in the week to discuss some kind of campus-wide memorial for the young man who always wore a color-coordinated outfit and was so proud of his job at Burger Chef. He said the mood around school was sad, as if students couldn't believe something so horrific could have happened.

"He was here one day and then gone the next," he said. "It's very depressing."

SURVIVING AND MOVING ON

After the funerals, the families of the four crew members tried to get on with the business of living, but it wasn't easy. Losing a child under any circumstance is difficult, but it is infinitely harder when that child's death is on the front page of the local paper every morning and the lead story on the television news each night. Although the authorities hoped to temper the amount of exposure the case received, interest in it was too great, and it led to a lot of discomfort for the families in mourning. All of them received crank phone calls and were victims of other forms of harassment that went on for days, weeks, months and years after the event. They routinely found well-wishers lurking on their doorsteps and curiosity seekers driving slowly down the street, and they were bombarded with false claims from publicity seekers looking for their fifteen minutes of fame.

The Sheltons began receiving disturbing phone calls before their daughter was buried and continued receiving those calls for an extended time afterward. Rachel said every time she answered the phone, there would be no one on the other end of the line. Police eventually traced the calls to local telephone booths, but it was impossible to know who actually made them. Pranksters rang the Shelton doorbell at all hours of the night only to disappear before being seen. However, the most unsettling event was a handwritten note they received from someone claiming to have vital information about the murder but who refused to disclose it out of fear that the individual involved would go to jail. The family turned the letter over to the authorities, but nothing came of it.

One family member, who was eleven at the time of the murders, remembered several instances in which Ruth's parents were harassed. She recalled the police showing up at the Sheltons' home and the phone company changing the number several times in an attempt to give the family peace. She said there were a number of cruel calls from so-called psychics who said they had contacted Ruth on the other side and wanted to tell Rachel what was said. She said it was next to impossible to find out who was behind the calls even though the phone line had a tap on it. "Remember, this was before caller ID," she said in a Facebook post.

Two weeks after her daughter's death, Carolyn Friedt spoke about Jayne to *Indianapolis Star* columnist Tom Keating. Carolyn recalled that the last time she saw Jayne was on November 16. She said the twenty-year-old was a young woman in the prime of her life. She had her own apartment. She had a job that she loved, and she enjoyed an active social life. As she sat on the edge of her mother's sofa for the last time playing with the family dog, Jayne apologized to her parents for not visiting very often but said that she'd been making regular trips to Terre Haute in order to help out her grandparents who had been ill.

"It was so like her," Friedt said.

Carolyn said the Speedway Police Department and other law enforcement agencies had been nothing but kind to all of the families and she was especially grateful to the FBI agent who brought her the news of Jayne's death, but she hoped whoever was responsible for killing her daughter would eventually be caught. She knew deep down she would be bitter if the individuals involved were not brought to justice, but she also knew harboring that bitterness was no way to honor Jayne's memory, so she tried to put any negative thoughts aside.

"It's difficult to do," she admitted.

It was also difficult not to focus on all the things she might have done differently if she knew her time with Jayne was limited. Carolyn said she

The grave of Jayne Friedt in Roselawn memorial cemetery in Terre Haute, Indiana. She is buried next to her brother who died in infancy. *Author's private collection.*

wished she'd spent more time with Jayne when she was younger or when she was involved in the Girl Scouts, but she would not have tried to shelter Jayne from the real world. In spite of what had happened, she hoped other parents would not keep their children under glass, prevent them from working at night or stop them from becoming independent individuals.

"You can't hide your children or protect them from the world. If you try, they will be vulnerable and naïve when the world finally reaches them," she said. "There have been times in the past when we have talked of getting away from the crime and violence in society and going to some remote area to live. But one reason we never left was because it wasn't right for our children. They had to learn about the world. We still feel that way."

A COMMUNITY ON EDGE

Authorities knew that the families of the Burger Chef murder victims were counting on them to find the killer or killers and put them behind bars, and they spared no expense to try to crack the case. In the early weeks of the investigation, there were approximately thirty officers working around the clock to try to solve the mysterious deaths. They gave up their Thanksgiving holidays and four-day weekends to pursue a variety of leads. They took notes on every call that came into the station. They encouraged anyone who ate at the Burger Chef on the night of the kidnappings to come forward, and they beefed up surveillance throughout the Speedway area.

Management at the Burger Chef restaurant on Crawfordsville Road noticed a considerable upswing in the number of police patrols around the store. The restaurant reopened on Saturday, November 25, and within the first three hours of operation, police toured the parking lot several times. But despite the increased security presence, business remained slow.

Store manager Robert Gilyeat also implemented a number of procedural changes in response to the crime. He ordered that the back door remain locked at all times and stated that the trash could only be removed during daylight business hours. The measures were designed to improve the safety of those who worked at the franchise and help them feel secure. Although crew members appreciated the extra effort, two female employees turned in their notices. One of them was Ginger Haggard, the young woman who traded shifts with Mark and avoided death by not being on the premises the week before. Gilyeat admitted that in light of recent events, he would probably have some difficulty replacing the employees.

The Speedway Burger Chef was not the only entity on edge in the days and weeks following the murders. The mood at area high schools was incredibly tense, especially those schools that lost one of their own. Speedway High School principal John Bainbridge said parents no longer presumed to know where their children were going or with whom they were hanging out. The kids themselves seemed more aware of their surroundings, quick to point out any suspicious activity and rethinking any after-school employment. "So many things have happened that the kids are very sensitive," he said. "Instead of just going out and getting a job, they stop and think."

A Northwest High School student who sat next to Ruth in algebra class said it was weird to face her empty desk the week after her funeral. "It was very strange the following Monday when she was not there," he said.

Principal George Gale said many of his students were apprehensive, not only the ones who had a personal connection to one of the victims. "I have never seen anything like this grip a community. Many people never experience two tragedies like this [the earlier bombings and murders] so close in a lifetime, yet these kids have seen both in the same school year," he said.

Compounding Complications

The weeks following the funerals were a difficult time not only for the families and the community but also for the law enforcement agencies that were investigating the incident in hopes of finding those responsible for the murders. With every day that passed, the case became more difficult to crack, and when reward money, public pleas and composite sketches failed to generate a solid lead, authorities commissioned clay busts to be made of the two men who were seen behind the Burger Chef restaurant the night of November 17. Three-dimensional models had been used with some success in Los Angeles, but it was the first time that a local agency employed such a method to try to solve a case. Lieutenant William Mahler said making the busts was a complicated process and not one that would be used on a regular basis. "It will only be used in major cases," he said. "We hope to save time on the investigation by using them to speed up the identification of the two men."

Robin England, a niece of one of the investigators and a Ball State University art student, was asked to help with the creation of the busts. She based her rendering on the descriptions provided to the police by the teenage eyewitnesses who were in the parking lot on the night of the abduction. The couple was brought in to examine the busts prior to their completion, and after making a few minor suggestions, they pronounced the finished product to be between 95 and 100 percent accurate. The models were featured in the newspaper and put on display at the Speedway Police Department.

In addition to relying on the recollections of the teenage couple and artistic abilities of England, authorities tapped into known criminal channels in pursuit of a hot tip. Their fishing produced a few early bites. There was someone who claimed to be in the Dunkin' Donuts that Friday night and allegedly saw someone accosting Mark Flemmonds next door. This individual also saw Ruth Ellen Shelton in a car a few minutes later as she was being abducted from the fast-food franchise. The witness was positive that the young lady in the car was Ruth Ellen because he knew the Northwest High School student well. It was unclear to detectives if the individual was merely an innocent bystander or possibly involved in the crime, but if true, it was another piece of the puzzle they didn't have before.

Without a doubt, the Burger Chef murder mystery was an unusually complicated case. According to Indiana State Police major Robert Allen, every day that went by with no word on the men in the composite sketches, they looked less like "people of interest" and more like potential suspects who were on the run or in hiding. To make matters worse, the fact that there were two crime scenes—twenty-two miles apart—compounded the difficulty of effectively searching for clues. Whenever there is distance involved, looking into suspicious incidents that may or may not be connected to the crime means covering a lot of territory.

One incident that had attracted some attention was an alleged shooting at Port Royale in northwest Johnson County, but authorities had no reason to believe it was connected to the Burger Chef murders.

A week after the crime, communication issues between the state police and the Johnson County Sheriff's Department seemed to have ebbed as well. Sheriff Tom Pritchard reiterated his offer to supply staff to assist troopers with their investigation, and Allen said he was grateful for their support. On Saturday, November 25, state police and about twenty volunteers used metal detectors to comb the murder scene at Stones Crossing Road. They found a number of trinkets, including nails, bottle caps, BBs and other debris, but no evidence that would help detectives working on the quadruple homicide.

After much of the onsite investigation was completed, Pritchard pledged his commitment to the case. "If there is any way we can help, we will," he said.

Authorities were discouraged. After re-investigating the Johnson County woods in hopes of finding any physical evidence that might have been missed the first time around, one question nagged at detectives working the case. There were a number of wooded areas between Speedway and the Heger property in which the killers could have carried out their heinous crime. Why hold out for such a remote location? There was only one reason that made any sense: most likely, the killers had some familiarity with both areas. Investigators began to look for a connection.

Chapter 6

LEADS, LOOK-ALIKES AND A LOT OF DEAD ENDS

F inding that connection would not be easy. The composite sketches and clay busts of the two men who were seen behind the Burger Chef on the night of the abductions resulted in 500 to 600 phone calls to the Speedway Police Department's special hotline phone number in the week following the murders. Approximately 192 of the informants supplied the name of someone who they felt matched the depictions, while an additional 150 calls came from those who felt confident they had seen one or both of the men but had no idea who they were.

In an effort to help police find those who were responsible for the murders, the *Indianapolis Star* created a special system so that the public could anonymously submit any leads or tips that they had on the case. The newspaper instructed its readers to write down their information on a piece of paper and then "sign" their tip with any six-digit numerical combination at the top and bottom of the page. The informant was then told to tear off the bottom half of the page and put the number in a safe place so that it could be used to identify them in the event that officials wanted to speak with them.

The letters poured in, but they varied wildly in content. Some were highly detailed while others, though well intentioned, were vague. Some writers offered up minor firsthand factoids that they didn't think would amount to much, while others placed their faith in "psychic visions" and dreams they had about the crime. None of the early letters offered up a decent lead, but police remained hopeful that one of them just might hold the key that would unlock the mystery. Although every piece of information received, whether on the phone or in writing, was dutifully typed on an index card and filed away for future reference, some tips received more attention than others. One Johnson County man reported that he saw a suspicious individual standing on Stone's Crossing Road on November 18. He said the person bore a striking resemblance to the "clean shaven man" in the composite sketches and offered to undergo hypnosis in order to remember additional details.

Another person alleged seeing a group of people standing near the murder site by what appeared to be a broken-down van and wondered if they might be involved. This seemingly innocuous tip was deemed significant because investigators believed that a van might have been used to transport the victims to their deaths.

Yet another individual told of an incident involving two men who matched the composites trying to shortchange a Greenwood gas station attendant in the early morning hours of November 18. Police spoke with the employee who was on duty that night and learned that the two men pulled up to the service station at U.S. 31 and County Line Road in a black Chevrolet and proceeded to purchase twelve dollars of fuel. The "bearded man" tried to pay for the gas with a five-dollar bill and two singles. When the clerk pointed out his mistake, the man went back to his car to get more money, and after paying for their gas, both men spewed obscenities at the employee before driving off, causing the attendant to wonder if they might have been on drugs.

"He [the bearded man] was all spaced out," the employee said.

Authorities considered the information but said it was highly unlikely that the suspects would draw attention to themselves so close to the place where they killed four people. It seemed far more probable that they were laying low or had left town.

On Sunday, November 26, numerous phone calls flooded police station switchboards after Chicago authorities arrested Danny White, thirty-six, and Danny Minigh, twenty-eight, following a disturbance at a local wedding party. The two, who were reported to be members of a Chicago street gang, were charged with aggravated battery for the beating and stabbing of officer Lawrence Eakles, a Chicago policeman, who was in a northwest-side pub enjoying a private celebration with his family and friends. The story was featured on a local late-night newscast and seen by viewers in northern Indiana who felt both individuals fit the general description of the bearded man the Speedway police were looking for. An investigator screened the footage and talked to the Chicago police in order to find out if there could be a connection but was told that one of the men had a solid alibi for his whereabouts on the night of the murders. The other man was deemed to be yet another look-alike as well.

"We're not going to Chicago to interview them," state police sergeant Charles H. Hibbert said.

Hot Tip in Cincy

Police did travel to Cincinnati to investigate another suspect who looked like the bearded man and was being held in connection with the robbery of an elderly woman. According to a source for the *Franklin Daily Journal*, the guy not only looked like the bearded man but was also named by another person as having something to do with the crime. The individual had lived within a few blocks of the Speedway Burger Chef at one time, but he was not in town on the night of the abduction and murders. He returned about two hours after the murders were thought to have taken place and went out of his way to immediately dye his hair and beard. Major Robert Allen called the lead "promising" but cautioned against anyone getting too excited about it. After all, it could be another dead end.

The Cincinnati informant, who passed a polygraph and had an alibi for his whereabouts on November 17, told the police that there were two others responsible for the murders. He said neither of the suspects intended to kill the hostages. The plan was to let the kids go after the robbery once their escape was assured; however, they were forced to silence the kids forever when Ruth Ellen Shelton recognized one of her captors.

Although authorities had no idea how the seventeen-year-old could have possibly known one of the suspects, they felt pretty good about the story. It fit the logical narrative of what they believed to have transpired. But a few days later, Hibbert announced that investigators were moving away from the Buckeye State.

He was concerned that the informant had an ulterior motive for his tip. Perhaps the individual was hoping to make a deal with authorities in exchange for his assistance, and even if he passed the lie detector test, it didn't mean his account was accurate—only that he believed what he was saying.

In actuality, investigators were far from optimistic that any of the look-alikes would pan out. At first glance, the composite drawings appeared to

THE BURGER CHEF MURDERS IN INDIANA

be highly detailed, but in reality, the hairstyles and features of the two men police were interested in speaking with were common in the late 1970s. In fact, a number of men who resembled the men in the sketches voluntarily reported to Speedway police headquarters to offer alibis as to where they were on the weekend of the murders. It wasn't that they felt guilty, but some said they had been getting a lot of curious looks from neighbors and co-workers ever since the composite pictures had been published.

In addition to looking into serious tips, police also had to investigate some of the more fantastic ones that came across their desks, including the report of a supposed abduction in which the kidnapper told his victim that he was involved in the Burger Chef murders. According to the tipster, he was hijacked as he was getting into his car at 4:00 a.m. on December 5 at the 1200 block of North Pennsylvania Street. The abductor forced him to drive to his own apartment, and during the trip, he confessed his participation in the crime. When they arrived at the individual's residence, he signed the title of his car over to his captor, who took the keys and a pistol from the apartment, as well as a few other possessions. The police had no idea if the story could have a shred of truth to it, but they admitted it could go either way.

In another incredible tale, a man checked into a Beech Grove motel claiming to be the uncle of one of the crew members. He presented an Alabama driver's license but registered under a Lafayette, Indiana address before changing it to the city of Lawrence. During his stay, he changed his story about being related to one of the victims and instead told motel employees that he was a detective working on the investigation. When he skipped out on the bill, management called the authorities, telling them that the man resembled the bearded man they were looking for. Officers ran his name through their system only to discover that the address he provided was nonexistent. From what the police could tell, the guy was not connected to any of the murder victims, but he did have a petty criminal record and because he mentioned the case, they wanted to speak with him. It was another lead that would go nowhere.

However, by the middle of December, investigators would be in possession of a letter that had the potential to break the case wide open—provided they could find the person who wrote it.

LETTER "-812"

Authorities were discouraged. In the three weeks since Jayne, Ruth, Mark and Daniel were kidnapped and subsequently killed, they were no closer to solving the Burger Chef murder mystery than they were on November 19. It was as though someone had committed the perfect crime, or one that was aided by mistakes made inside the police departments and a strange twist of fate that may have prevented authorities from having a living witness to the incident.

According to Mark Flemmonds's death certificate, the coroner determined that the young man had several lacerations and blows to his head, but those contusions were not the cause of his death. While Mark may have sustained a beating on the night of the murders (as police believed), the beating didn't kill him. What seemed most likely was the possibility that Mark ran into a tree while trying to escape his captors and knocked himself out. The position in which he landed caused the blood to drain into his lungs and caused him to choke. Had he landed in any other position, he might have passed out for a period of time, but he would have regained consciousness. In fact, the pathology report said that Mark was alive approximately five to twenty minutes after hitting the tree. (Later reports would insist that Mark died of injuries resulting from a beating with a blunt object or a chain.)

It was a crucial fact that helped round out the overall narrative as to what might have taken place. Investigators were now convinced that something went awry—first at the restaurant when a simple robbery resulted in abduction but also at the murder scene. They believed that after shooting Ruth and Daniel, the killers lost control of the situation when the other two jumped up and ran for their lives. Although they recaptured Jayne right away and stabbed her, it was possible that they could not find Mark and assumed he got away. Police theorized that if the killers knew Mark was passed out somewhere nearby, they would have ensured his silence. Instead, when they thought one of their victims might have lived to tell the tale, they fled the scene as quickly as possible. It was one of several possible scenarios but one that made the most sense to those who were studying it.

On November 29, the *Indianapolis Star* received a letter from a tipster that more or less confirmed that theory. It was written in blue ink on a page from a secretarial notebook and signed with a six-digit number ending in "-812." The letter alleged that there were three individuals involved in the crime, and as authorities suspected, the caper started out as a basic robbery and then took a turn. The letter did not explain why the robbers decided to kill the crew members, but the writer admitted that one suspect fired the shots that killed Ruth and Daniel while another was responsible for stabbing Jayne. The third person on the scene was allegedly a bystander who stayed in the car the entire time and was taken by surprise when the incident ended in murder. "I am not the third person, but I do know this person would give up and confess if you people promised immunity. The third person does not want your money, just immunity. But I would like to have it." The letter also confirmed what police already suspected: that those who were responsible for the murders had split up and were no longer in the state of Indiana.

It was just the kind of break the police were hoping for—assuming it was true. Authorities were eager to speak to the person behind the paper, and they made several public pleas for him or her to come forward. It was nearly two weeks before a follow-up letter arrived, but before authorities could respond to it, another credible tip made its way into the station. Someone claiming to have "important and confidential information" about the case wrote it and enclosed a torn one-dollar bill so that they could be identified as the author in the event investigators and detectives wanted to talk to him.

Before the police could hold a press conference to ask the writer to come forward, the man dropped by the *Indianapolis Star* newsroom to chat with reporters. He seemed nervous throughout his interview and repeatedly claimed that his life was in danger if his identity were to be revealed. Staff writers assured the man that his anonymity would be protected provided they could share his contact information with the authorities. The man agreed, and a phone call was arranged. Lieutenant William Crafton also met with the individual for over an hour in his home.

The new informant contradicted the author of letter "-812" by saying there were only two suspects involved in the murders: a ringleader who had a long rap sheet that included three arrests for murder and several convictions for robbery and burglary; and a drug addict who was already well known to the police and had a history of extreme violence. Both men bore a striking resemblance to the composite drawings and most likely committed the murder in order to have some dirt on each other and to establish a bond of mutual trust.

The man said he'd known both men since 1970 and provided the authorities with a number of details that might be helpful: their names, last known addresses, the kinds of cars they drove and more. He said that they were known for luring young women into prostitution at truck stops and frequenting local strip clubs. Although the informant originally eschewed the idea of claiming the proffered reward from the Burger Chef corporation, he later recanted: "I have talked about it with my relatives and we decided we want the money."

There were two more names to look into, but officers were far from confident that they would lead to anything. They were far more interested in the second letter that arrived from the mysterious "-812." Once again, the note was printed in blue ink on the same kind of secretarial notebook paper as before, but this time it opened with an ominous admission: "I don't think I will be able to help anymore."

> *But you got to believe that the third person didn't know what was going to happen to the four kids when they arrive in the woods. They was going to just tie them up and leave. Supposedly there was nothing said about killing them.*
>
> *The third person try to stop them and supposedly…after the first child was shot, the third person* [yelled "run"] *and got beat up for it. I wish the one that ran into the tree didn't died, that way maybe you police men would have these killers locked up by now.*

The writer confirmed that the three were no longer together and had not seen one another since that fateful night. They refused to reveal the name of the third person involved because they truly believed their version of events and did not want to see that individual get into any trouble. They said they hoped that the inmate in Cincinnati might know who one of the other suspects was and would be able to supply additional information without getting the third person in the middle of it. "I'm sorry I can't help any more than this, but I can't break a promise," the letter concluded.

Police weren't sure what might entice the individual to say more. For several days, they made public appeals, promising the third suspect immunity in exchange for their cooperation, but no one came forward. Police had to admit that the informant's story might be nothing more than a tall tale. Overall, they were disheartened. Although there were still some avenues to explore before throwing in the towel or admitting defeat, they could not deny that the trail was starting to grow cold and they may never know who was responsible for the murder. However, they continued plugging along, hoping to find that one clue or piece of evidence that would solve the mystery once and for all.

In Need of Closure

As the number of leads ebbed, authorities had no choice but to reevaluate the amount of time and resources being dedicated to the Burger Chef case. On December 5, the special hotline created to take calls from the public twenty-four hours a day was turned off between midnight and 8:00 a.m. Officers were slowly reassigned to their regular duties, and the coalition of agencies closed their joint offices at the Speedway Police Department. Indiana State Police major Robert Allen was quick to assure the public that no one was giving up hope that the case would be resolved, but it was only natural, after a certain period, to reprioritize goals and give those who had been working so tirelessly on the investigation a chance to rest.

The news of this reevaluation was especially hard on the aggrieved parents who were in desperate need of closure. On the one-month anniversary of their daughter's death, George and Carolyn Friedt went public with an emotionally charged appeal for anyone with any information regarding the case to go to the police:

> *We speak only for ourselves and not for the other parents of the other children who were kidnapped and viciously murdered on the eve of November 17th and the morning of November 18th....In the investigation it is evident that many people have tried to help by telling the police what they have seen and overheard in and around the area of the kidnappings. For this we are grateful to all.* [However,] *as police now retrace their steps and look again, it is quite evident that some people who were near or in the restaurant that night have not come forward....We hope some will....Help take these killers off the streets before they strike again.*

The couple also encouraged Burger Chef to reduce its $25,000 reward by $1,000 each day in hopes that the diminished sum would compel someone to speak up with any critical information they may have. They believed it had been long enough and anyone hoping to claim the money no longer deserved the full amount.

Burger Chef spokesperson Richard Bolinger said if the police agreed that a reward reduction was in order, he would follow that recommendation, but so far, it had not been suggested. In past cases, it had been shown that a reward could attract information months down the road, especially if a suspect's situation had changed. If someone suddenly needed an influx of cash, for example, they might be willing to spill the beans. "With our reward, we want to do the best we can to attract that information," he said.

Even Indianapolis mayor William Hudnut III felt that the window of opportunity may be closing on finding the people who were responsible for the murders, and he urged the public to speak out if they had any information that could help. "Please, step forward and do your duty as a citizen. There must be somebody, somewhere who knows something that will lead to a solution of this awful crime."

But whoever that someone might be, one thing was clear: they weren't talking.

Chapter 7

A NEW YEAR

A uthorities took a break from the Burger Chef case over the holidays but resumed their investigation in January 1979. They were recharged and reenergized, and there was hope that the new year would lead to new developments that would help resolve the case and bring peace of mind to the families, police and community at large. In an effort to help, the *Indianapolis Star* reached out to a psychologist at Central State Hospital in hopes that a behavioral specialist may be able to provide a window into the minds of the murderers in order to determine what kind of person could commit such an act.

Based on the available evidence, the psychologist suspected the men behind the murders were probably on drugs at the time of the crime and may have been willing to kill for a thrill—especially if they happened to be recognized by one of their victims. The specialist speculated that the men might have been under the influence of phencyclidine (PCP), an animal tranquilizer known as "angel dust" on the street that has serious behavioral effects on those who use it. In addition to hallucinations, PCP can also infuse a person with tremendous strength, which can result in violent outbursts. Once the drug wears off and the individuals realize what has occurred, they typically have no remorse for their actions. In fact, it's rare if they talk about them at all.

However, PCP was not the only type of substance that could result in criminal behavior. "Alcohol by itself could cause the same violent effect," the psychologist said. "I've known glue sniffers who will do wild, crazy things."

The specialist was also given a copy of the two letters sent by the writer known as "-812." The specialist agreed that those responsible for the murder most likely left the state, but he believed that at some point, the author of the letters would make himself or herself known.

"That's one hell of a load to carry, but I believe that person may also be involved or has a special relationship with at least one of the suspects involved," he said, alluding that the individual may be a lover or drinking or drug buddy of one of the murderers.

The state police reached out to a psychoanalyst as well in order to get an opinion of the type of people they might be looking for. Their specialist concluded that the murderers were probably unproductive men between the ages of sixteen and twenty-five and that one of them could be considered a psychopath. By definition, a psychopath is a clinically insane individual who kills in a trancelike state. It seemed unlikely that there was more than one psychopath involved, as they do not tend to travel in pairs.

The psychoanalyst did not rule out the possibility of the murders being carried out by a sociopath, but the crime didn't fit the nature of that particular profile. Although sociopaths are considered to be of sound mind and the kind of person who knows the difference between right and wrong, they have a complete disregard for the rules. At their core, they are con artists who know how to turn on the charm in order to get what they want rather than resorting to brute force. They also do not tend to go to a lot of trouble to commit their crimes. If the Burger Chef incident was supposed to be a simple robbery, a sociopath would have taken the money and left, even if he were recognized by one of the employees. A sociopath, by his very nature, would assume that he could beat the rap.

The fact that the perpetrators seemed in need of some ready cash and were willing to leave behind other items of value caused the psychologist to return to the drug theory. If the suspects were under the influence at the time of the incident and needed money for more drugs, it would explain their leaving so much behind, as well as their uncontrolled act of violence.

Could drugs have been involved somehow? Did one of the victims recognize their killers, and would the police ever find out who they were? The psychologist thought so. He believed that at some point, the killers would give themselves away, one would turn on the other or they would be caught for a similar crime. "[That] may be the only way they will be tracked," the psychologist noted.

THE LEADS DWINDLE

For two months, the *Indianapolis Star* published a near daily update on the case, as well as a tally of how many days had passed since the murder and the address of the reward desk so that anyone with information could submit his or her tips. However, on January 17, 1979, the paper decided to discontinue the daily reminder. It assured the public that the case remained an open investigation and that it would keep the public apprised of any new developments, but it was time for reporters to focus on other stories as well.

The murders were not out of the spotlight for long. By the end of the month, police announced that they were looking into several new suspects, including a man in Milwaukee, Wisconsin, and three men in the Indianapolis area who may or may not have been involved in the crime. They were quick to tell the public that no arrests had been made, no arrests were imminent and it was unclear if they could put any of the suspects in Speedway on the night of the abduction.

One of the men was of particular interest to authorities. He was already in the Marion County Jail on federal firearms charges, but he seemed to know more about the murders than most. He and the two other men grew up in Johnson County and were familiar with the area where the bodies were found. One of the men lived in White River Township, making him intimately familiar with the terrain, and it was suspected that they were not only involved in drug trafficking but they may have also been behind other fast-food heists in the past.

Authorities subjected the man in prison to a polygraph test, which showed he definitely had some firsthand knowledge about the case and had not simply gleaned information from the newspaper or daily broadcasts. Unfortunately, the test could not tell whether he was directly involved. Before they could question him further, the suspect's attorney advised against his participation. The other two men were also questioned, but the police were quick to tell reporters that they were among many who were under scrutiny.

"We have other people who are not as fresh as the fallen snow who are also being investigated," said one of the police officers working the case.

In March, the Burger Chef case was rocked when authorities announced that they were looking into possible connections between the slayings of the four fast-food workers, the coldblooded killing of Julia Scyphers and the Speedway bombings, which occurred within months of one another. There were those who already wondered if the three events could be related, but those suspicions were heightened when investigators noticed a similarity between the men depicted in the composite sketches and known mug shots of Brett Kimberlin and William Bowman.

Bowman, who was believed to be the man who gunned down Scyphers in the garage of her Speedway home, was jailed on February 28, the same day that a thirty-four-count federal indictment was handed down against Kimberlin charging him with the September bombing spree and a handful of other offenses. The two were known associates who were arrested together on February 19 in Corpus Christi, Texas, for attempting to import several tons of marijuana from Mexico. Police knew that Kimberlin was the former employer of Scyphers's daughter, and after Bowman was identified as the man who showed up at the Scypherses' front door on the day Julia was killed, it was suspected that Kimberlin might have sent him to do the deed. Police also believed that the subsequent bombings were designed to distract authorities from the Scyphers investigation, but what about the Burger Chef murders? How did they fit into Kimberlin's plan?

When reporters asked Marion County prosecutor Stephen Goldsmith to comment on the rumors that the events were interrelated, he demurred, saying he planned to meet with the two men in order to find out more. "I don't want to speculate," he said. "I just don't know."

The following day, however, Goldsmith, Speedway Police chief Robert Copeland and the Indiana State Police concluded that while the Scyphers murder and the bombings were most likely related and that Kimberlin and Bowman were linked to each other via the Scyphers incident, there was no evidence that the men were involved in the Burger Chef murders. They only considered the possibility because there had been so few solid leads in the case and they didn't want to leave any stone unturned.

A STRONG POSSIBILITY

Even though authorities were unwilling to link Kimberlin and Bowman to the quadruple homicide, they were willing to draw a connection between the men who were seen outside the restaurant by a teenage couple on the night of the abduction. For months, police backed away from naming the unknown men as suspects, preferring to say that they were only wanted for questioning. However, when the men never came forward to explain their presence near the restaurant, authorities could only conclude that they were involved somehow and that they probably cased the place several times that night before pulling off their crime.

But how did police know that the men had been watching the restaurant? State police investigator Ken York was pursuing a lead that involved two Johnson County men and a southern Marion County man who had been involved in a number of recent fast-food robberies. He had received a tip that on November 18, a man in a Greenwood bar boasted to other patrons about his involvement in the Burger Chef robbery. He even went so far as to say that the kids were abandoned in the country, where they would be found the following day. York and fellow detective Richard Bumps confronted the Greenwood man and questioned him.

"His exact words to Dick and me were 'I knew I shot my mouth off at the wrong time,'" York said.

Virgil Vandagriff also spoke with the braggart, who all but confessed his involvement during a game of pool. The man said he was involved with several others who were in the habit of robbing area fast-food restaurants by hiding behind the dumpster and waiting for a night shift employee to take out the trash. That's when they would pull out a gun, rob the store of its ready cash and make a quick getaway. The plan on November 17 was to rob a Burger Chef on the east side of town, tie up the employees and leave, but that plan was thwarted when the suspects saw a police car in the parking lot. Nervous about participating in his first robbery, the Greenwood man got drunk, and the other suspect took him back to Franklin, where he picked up the others and drove out to the Speedway store in order to carry out the deed. He was ultimately taken into custody for questioning but was released after he passed a polygraph.

Bumps and York compared the reported timeline to the one from the night of the abduction and found that they matched. The pair then drove to Franklin in hopes of confronting one of the suspects, only to find him outside working in his yard. When Bumps saw the man, he did a double-take. He looked at the photo of the clay busts and then back at the man. "This guy in Franklin was a dead ringer for the bearded man," York said.

The individual denied all knowledge of the murders and said that any resemblance between him and the composite model was a coincidence. Investigators followed the trail to the second suspect, a fair-haired man who lived in the northwest portion of Johnson County, but he, too, denied any involvement. There was no evidence linking them to the crime scene, but the resemblance was uncanny, and neither had an alibi to account for their whereabouts on the night in question. The detectives were convinced that they had found the men responsible for the murders, but Johnson County prosecutor Charles D. Gantz was hesitant to authorize an arrest without more evidence linking them to the crime.

Gantz was a seasoned prosecutor who knew what it took to get a conviction beyond a reasonable doubt. Although there were a lot of strong emotions in a case such as this one, he knew a jury would not find someone guilty based on little more than a prosecutor's hunch and circumstantial evidence.

"I didn't think I could rule them out as suspects, but there are so many people in so vicious a crime as this who could have done it. I just didn't feel there were sufficient facts. You need to have proof that whoever is accused actually did do this crime," Gantz said.

When federal authorities arrested the Franklin man for possession of a weapon, a felony considering his previous record, detectives hoped he might confess his involvement in the Burger Chef murders—especially if he was not directly responsible for the crime itself. Despite the offers of leniency, he remained mum on the case. His White River Township running mate stayed silent as well.

"We could never crack them," York said.

As the days, weeks and months passed, police continued to look for leads in cases that occurred locally, regionally and throughout the country. They were especially interested in events that occurred in restaurants, if the victims were shot execution style, if the suspects ever lived in the Speedway area/were known to be in the Speedway area at the time of the murders or if those involved resembled the composite sketches. The Johnson County men remained the best lead in the Burger Chef murder mystery until April 1979, when police announced that two Massachusetts men were being held in Milwaukee on robbery-murder charges that seemed eerily similar to the Speedway case.

According to reports, Steven Coffey, twenty-seven, and Norman Pepin, twenty-four, of Somerville, Massachusetts, were arrested in a Chicago motel room after trying to cash $300 in stolen traveler's checks. The checks were connected to an engineer who had traveled to Milwaukee to take part in a professional conference. While there, he and two other men met Coffey and Pepin at a Holiday Inn and went with the men to a disco. At the end of the evening, instead of taking the trio back to their motel, the pair pulled off I-94, where they robbed them and forced them to lie facedown in a ditch where they were shot. Rogers Weeks, forty-six, of Glenora, California, and John Brutcher, twenty-five, of Louisville, Kentucky, were killed. The third man survived.

In addition to carrying out a similar execution to the Burger Chef case, when Coffey's and Pepin's mug shots were published, it was obvious that the pair bore more than a passing resemblance to the men in the composite sketches. But so did Kimberlin and Bowman, proving that a resemblance alone was not enough to charge them with the crime. As a result, the pair did not encourage detectives. Sergeant Charles Hibbert said the state police were unwilling to travel to Milwaukee to talk to the men who were already wanted in their home state for passing bad checks, larceny, conspiracy and receiving a stolen car.

"This indicates to me that it may be an investigative lead, but if it was a trail that was exceptionally strong, I'm sure we would not be waiting, and our people would be in Milwaukee right now," he said.

By May 1, police announced that Coffey and Pepin were no longer people of interest in the Burger Chef case. It seemed that every credible lead they pursued only led to one dead end after another.

A Vote of No Confidence

By the fall of 1979, the one-year anniversary of the Scyphers murder and Speedway bombings had passed without anyone being formally charged for either crime, and with the one-year anniversary of the Burger Chef case looming, it was obvious that a change was in order. On October 2, the Metropolitan Board of Police Commissioners met and unanimously voted to fire Speedway police chief Robert L. Copeland for his "lack of leadership." Copeland, who was at the helm of all three unsolved investigations, was given the opportunity to resign rather than face dismissal, but he refused, forcing the board's hand. Board president Joseph Eke said the decision was a long time in coming.

Problems within the department had been going on for at least two years. In late 1977, more than two hundred officers petitioned the board asking for Copeland's dismissal, and there were also reports of low morale and a high turnover rate within the agency. Couple those complaints with three unsolved mysteries, and the board felt it had no choice.

"The problems that led to this have been going on for a long, long time," Eke said. "There's general apathy in the department, a breakdown in the chain of command that's prevented us from carrying out our responsibilities. He's been aware that we were concerned."

Captain William R. Burgan was tapped to assume Copeland's duties until a new chief was named, but a change in leadership did not mean that there would be significant progress in the Burger Chef case. The trail was beginning to grow cold, and it had taken a toll on those who were involved in the investigation. A few weeks after the murders, Indiana State Police sergeant Richard Bumps discovered that he still had the identification of one of the victims in his coat pocket and found himself in hot water when he tried to return it.

It was an honest mistake, and when he realized he had it, he immediately contacted state police head evidence technician W. Sherrill Alspach and Detective Sergeant Ronald L. Bruce to turn in the items. The three agreed to meet at Jerry's Restaurant in Speedway, where Alspach and Bruce were planning to meet Terry Collinsworth and Barry Turner, two troopers assigned to the Johnson County end of the case, in order to compare notes. As Alspach, Bruce, Collinsworth and Turner sat in the restaurant awaiting Bumps's arrival, Indiana State Police captain Lloyd Monroe drove up and reprimanded the men for violating a department regulation prohibiting state police officers from taking a "coffee break" at certain times of the day. The idea was to keep as many troopers on the road during rush hour traffic as possible, and when Bumps saw Monroe's car in the parking lot, he knew he would be in trouble if he joined the group. Instead, he left the scene.

Alspach retired not long after the incident, but Bumps stayed the course, eventually suffering from a nervous breakdown and having to take an extended leave of absence. The turnover rate of investigators involved in the case was high in the year following the crime. It took its toll on the people who were heavily involved in the case and frustrated them that it had not been solved. In addition to Bumps and Alspach excusing themselves from the case, Lieutenant William Crafton was transferred soon after Robert Copeland's dismissal. He was no longer the head of detectives for the Speedway police force; he was now commander of the department's uniformed men. Major Robert Allen, who was the head of investigations for the Indiana State Police, retired in May 1979 to take a less stressful job with the Cummins Engineering Company in Columbus.

Despite the attrition rate, the investigation continued, and a year after the Burger Chef murders, Sergeant Brook Appleby and Trooper Don Lindsay were the only two original investigators still working the case on a full-time basis. It was quite a switch from the swarm of officials who were involved only twelve months before, but the duo did not mind the reduced numbers. If anything, it made their job a little bit easier.

On November 15, 1979, authorities held a press conference to give the public an update on their investigation. Area newspapers heavily publicized the event, and there was speculation that police would highlight the top leads in the case. However, it failed to live up to the hype. After one year of countless tips, a number of credible leads and a nonstop search into the events that occurred on November 17 and 18, 1978, there were no official suspects in the quadruple homicide.

Police assured the public that the investigation was ongoing and their commitment to it remained strong. They maintained a positive attitude that one day, the case would be resolved, but blanket statements backed by boilerplate soundbites were of little comfort to the families of those who were slain, such as Carolyn Friedt, who had lost hope that the police would find out who murdered her daughter.

"I'm very disappointed....It's especially hard to confront a tragedy like this. I still haven't had time to properly grieve for my daughter," she said.

Chapter 8

SIBLINGS, SOURCES AND SEVERAL NEW SUSPECTS

As 1979 faded into 1980, authorities continued to pursue leads in the Burger Chef murder mystery. Although leads did not come in at the same rate as they once did, investigators said that they still received several calls a week regarding the case and they were committed to examining every tip that might help add yet another piece to the puzzle.

In an effort to streamline the number of people working the case on a full-time basis, the law enforcement coalition created a seven-man task force to field calls and chase down any new theories. Under the leadership of Indiana State Police sergeant Leon Griffith, the task force was composed of state police detectives Ken York, Brooke Appleby and Jim Cramer; Indianapolis Police Department officer John Hruban; Lieutenant Buddy Ellwanger of the Speedway Police Department; and Sergeant Carold Baker of the Marion County Sheriff's Department. It was hoped that by creating this task force, the men would be able to pool their resources, concentrate their efforts and resolve the case once and for all.

A SMOKING GUN

Within weeks after its formation, it appeared the team's efforts were producing results. In February, the task force announced that it was re-investigating a twenty-four-year-old psychiatric patient who lived in

An architectural drawing for a 1980s-style Burger Chef. Note the Happy Bonnet Face sign has been replaced by the chef's hat outline. A restaurant of this style was located in Zionsville, Indiana, before Hardee's bought out the Burger Chef chain in the middle of the decade. *Indiana Historical Society Bass Collection.*

Greenwood at one time and could be placed in White River Township the day before the murders. On November 17, 1978, the suspect was stopped by a Speedway police officer for running over a curb around the time that the Burger Chef was being robbed. The officer questioned the driver but did not arrest him. It was only later that the authorities realized he had discarded a .38-caliber pistol near 21st Street and Cunningham Road, which was found over the weekend of the murders and traced back to its owner.

It could have been a coincidence, of course, but it gave investigators pause because the owner was a known associate of a convicted armed robber who lived one floor above Mark Flemmonds at the Big Eagle apartment complex. The complex was just yards away from the place where the former Greenwood resident was stopped by the police and where his weapon was jettisoned. Although the armed robber was not a friend of the Burger Chef employee, he knew Mark through pickup basketball games and was known to frequent the Crawfordsville Road franchise. Was it possible that Mark met the Greenwood man in passing? If he, too, was a regular at the Burger Chef, perhaps his face was familiar to others who worked there.

Sources with knowledge about the case said once the restaurant was robbed, those involved most likely forced Jayne Friedt to use her car to drive away from the Burger Chef in order to rendezvous with the getaway car. They suspected that Mark and Daniel Davis got into the back seat of the Vega while Ruth Ellen Shelton and the suspects crowded in the front with Jayne. (This theory was based on the statements of those who claimed to have seen the girls in a car on the night of the abduction.) After they met up with the others on 15th Street, the kids were transferred into another car or van for the ride to Johnson County.

Not long after the murders, authorities learned that their Greenwood suspect had sought counseling for some personal issues, and when they compelled him to take a lie detector test, it indicated that he was less than truthful on several of his answers. Unfortunately, investigators were prevented from interrogating him further when he retained an attorney who advised him against speaking to the police or answering any more questions regarding the Burger Chef case.

Detectives admitted that the Greenwood gunman was a prime suspect, but he was not the only one the task force was looking at in connection with the crime. They were also interested in two men who were responsible for robbing several fast-food franchises and convenience stores in Marion and Johnson Counties since 1976. Two of those robberies included Burger Chef restaurants.

Timothy L. Piccione, twenty-six, and John W. Defibaugh, twenty-nine, admitted to robbing the Burger Chef restaurants at 444 East Sumner and 1632 East Southport Road using methods that were eerily similar to the Speedway incident. In both cases, the men accosted crew members in the parking lot after the stores closed and forced them back into the restaurant at gunpoint. After compelling one of the crew members to open the safe and robbing the place of its ready cash, they forced the employees to lie facedown on the floor, where they tied them up prior to making their escape. In at least one of the robberies, the men shot one of their victims and stabbed another.

Piccione had been on detectives' radar early in the investigation, along with a twenty-seven-year-old Franklin resident who was arrested on an unrelated firearms charge. Defibaugh was also mentioned as a possible suspect in connection with the crime along with another Franklin man, but nothing panned out. Now police wanted a second look at the pair, especially after they seized a station wagon owned by Defibaugh that matched the description of one that was seen near the Burger Chef at the time of the abduction. Defibaugh was quick to tell authorities that he recently purchased the vehicle and had nothing to do with the Speedway crime. Piccione denied involvement as well. The pair submitted to polygraph tests, which helped to clear up a number of unsolved crimes the duo was responsible for, but they could not prove that the pair had anything to do with the murders of four Burger Chef crew members in the fall of 1978.

Despite the continued setbacks, the members of the task force refused to give up. After interviewing more than one thousand people about the case and reviewing the twenty binders filled with information and leads, they remained hopeful that they would eventually find those responsible.

"I feel it in my heart that we will solve this case and make an arrest," Lindsay said.

A Reliable Source

An arrest appeared to be imminent in October, when authorities announced that they had a firm suspect in the case and reason to believe that drugs may have been involved. Although investigators would not speculate as to when the arrest might be made, they said that they had received information from a reliable source that not only confirmed the known facts of the case but also offered additional details that implicated an individual who had been on their radar as early as November 19, 1978.

Jim Cramer said the tipster's information was solid and that he had no reason to doubt him or her. "We know who one [of the murderers] was," he said. "I have no doubts in my mind the suspect can be placed in the woods in Johnson County at the time of the murders."

In addition, authorities asserted that the four Burger Chef employees might have been killed over a $7,000 drug debt. This claim stemmed from a conversation Mark Flemmonds had with an acquaintance the night before he died. He told his associate that he'd amassed a significant debt with a local drug pusher and was afraid he might be killed if he did not square his account.

The $7,000 sum sounded steep for a high school student, unless he was a dealer as well. But even if the amount was exaggerated in an effort to sound impressive to a friend, police were not surprised to learn that drugs may have been a factor in the crime. They knew the Crawfordsville Road Burger Chef was frequented by a number of well-known drug traffickers, including some with ties to large international cartels. In fact, in the months prior to the murders, the Speedway police had monitored the restaurant for drug-related activity after receiving reports that narcotics were being sold out the back door and in the restrooms. Officials at Burger Chef's corporate office said they were unaware such transactions were taking place on store property, but at least a few employees knew about the sales. Was it possible that they took part in such deals as well?

Maybe. Not only was there some evidence to suggest that Mark may have dabbled in marijuana, but traces of the substance were found in Jayne Friedt's system, according to her autopsy report. Could it be that a botched drug deal led to the deaths of the four young people?

Police refused to speculate, but they couldn't ignore the evidence. Armed with information from their reliable source, the rumor that Mark may have owed money to a pusher and the traces of pot in Jayne's bloodstream gave them reason to believe that their prime suspect was a former Johnson County resident with a long criminal history of selling narcotics in both Indianapolis and Speedway.

Ken York insisted that this was not a new suspect but one of hundreds of people who resembled one of the men depicted in the composite sketches. He said if the information they received from the tipster was valid, it would prove his theory that at least one of the killers had to be familiar with rural Johnson County.

"To me, I always thought someone had to know where that place was. They didn't just stumble across it," he said. "I was always working on the theory that it had to be someone with Johnson County ties."

But investigators faced a big problem when it came to making an arrest: the suspect was no longer in the state. After learning that he was wanted on criminal theft charges, the suspect flew to Florida, where he was eventually arrested for burglary. He was released from jail on bond and immediately jumped state again. He resurfaced in Texas, where the FBI caught up with him on October 31, 1980. Federal agents took both the suspect and his common-law wife into custody, and Indiana authorities wasted no time in traveling to the Lone Star State. They hoped to speak to the suspect to find out exactly what role he may have played in the Speedway slayings, but Texas law prevented them from doing so.

They were able to take custody of the man's lover and returned her to Indiana, where she was held at the Marion County Jail on a $25,000 bond. They assumed the suspect would remain incarcerated in Texas until he could be extradited to the Hoosier State, but while they were waiting for the paperwork to wind its way through the legal process, he was released from prison on yet another bond and disappeared.

Cramer was not rattled by the man's release. "He'll be back in jail," he said, noting that the man was only one of several people the authorities were looking at in connection to the Burger Chef murders. "We intend to keep working on this....We're still pushing to keep it [the investigation] going until we find the murderers."

A DIRECT LINK

After two years of tirelessly and doggedly looking at every shred of evidence that came their way, authorities had yet to make an arrest in the Burger Chef case. The suspect in Texas was ultimately cleared of any involvement in the crime, but investigators remained confident that drugs were a probable motive for the robbery turned murder. Five months later, an incident occurred that not only fueled this speculation but also gave the community its first direct link between the slain employees and those who traded in illegal drugs.

On March 5, 1981, James W. Friedt, the brother of the murdered Burger Chef assistant manager, was arrested with two other men for selling thirty grams of cocaine. For all intents and purposes, it was a routine charge that shouldn't have made any waves, but when folks saw James's mug shot, which was published in the *Indianapolis Star*, they couldn't help notice a resemblance between Jayne's sibling and the "bearded man" who was pictured in the composite drawings.

It was an unfair comparison that reached James in his Marion County Jail cell. When he heard the rumor, he was shocked and sickened by the idea that he could have had something to do with his sister's murder. Not only did he deny the allegation that he was one of the now infamous suspects, but he also denounced the idea that Jayne was a heavy drug user. "I'm not saying she didn't try it [drugs], but the smell of marijuana made her sick and she would not allow it to be smoked around her."

James told detectives working the case that the last time he saw his sister alive was approximately a week before she was killed. He said he'd been in the Crawfordsville Road Burger Chef on November 17, 1978, but he did not see Jayne or the other three victims while he was on the premises.

James's arrest was already difficult for the Friedt family, but the reports loosely linking his arrest and drug activity to Jayne's murder sent everyone over the edge. James reported that the rumor caused neighbors to harass his parents and his mother was so emotionally distraught over the whole thing that she refused to speak to him.

Friedt believed that the murders were most likely related to a botched robbery and speculated that when his sister was held up at the restaurant's back door, perhaps Mark Flemmonds came to her aid. He also believed that Mark Flemmonds may have been the first to die and that the killers needed to eliminate all potential witnesses. It was a startling theory from a victim's family member, but it was unclear how he arrived at this conclusion or if it was a purely speculative guess.

Lieutenant Larry Charmichael emphatically denied that James was in any way connected to the murder case. He told the press that Jayne's brother had been positively eliminated as a possible suspect or accomplice in the crime. "There are several aspects we are still investigating, but right now, we don't have anything of value," he said.

James Friedt was not the only Burger Chef sibling to run afoul of the law. In May 1982, Kevin M. Flemmonds, twenty-three, and three of his associates were charged with the December 24, 1981 robbery and murder of Adrian A. Brown, a known drug dealer who lived on the 2700 block of Dearborn Street.

On the night of Brown's death, Kevin and his friends kicked things off with the holdup of a Wake-Up filling station at 1500 East 34th Street, and then they robbed a man in the 3700 block of North Oxford before proceeding to Brown's house with the intention of robbing him of his drug stash. When they arrived, one of the men entered Brown's residence under the pretense of making a buy while the others waited outside. When Brown went to retrieve the drugs from their hiding place, the accomplice let Kevin and the other men inside in order to ambush the dealer. Brown was hit with three bullets from three different weapons, one of which was traced back to Kevin. He stood trial and was convicted of conspiracy to commit murder, murder and robbery. He was sentenced to twenty-five years for each charge.

Once again, there was speculation that Kevin's involvement in the local drug scene may have had a direct or indirect impact on Mark's death, but authorities didn't believe so. It was merely a coincidence. However, in 2007, the rumor was resurrected when investigators got a match on a partial palmprint they lifted from Jayne Friedt's Vega. At the time of the murders, police did not have the capability to compare prints across a large database, but nearly three decades later, technology caught up to the crime.

Trooper William Stoney Vann, who inherited the case in 1998, was ecstatic about the hit. "I was on cloud nine. This was a big lead. This could break the case wide open," he said.

The print belonged to a man who had been arrested for several misdemeanors and was a fringe friend of Kevin Flemmonds's at one time. It seemed almost too perfect that one partial palmprint would connect all the dots, and as it turned out, it was. After sitting down for an interview with authorities and agreeing to a polygraph test, the man in question was cleared of any involvement in the crime. No one could say for certain how his palmprint ended up on Jayne's car, but perhaps he brushed up against the vehicle in the Burger Chef parking lot or in another public place at some point. Palmprints can only confirm that someone has touched a particular item. They can't say when they touched it, why they may have touched it or if they were doing anything illegal when they did.

But back in 1982, the Burger Chef murder mystery once again appeared to be at a dead end.

Chapter 9

AN INMATE WITH INFORMATION

On a cold, gray afternoon in December 1984, *Indianapolis Star* reporter Dan Luzadder made his way through the crowds of holiday shoppers on his way to meet an inmate at the Marion County Jail. The individual had called the newsroom earlier that day to say that he was facing habitual theft charges and was in need of some help. He told Luzadder that he had a hot tip that might make for an interesting story and was willing to exchange it for any assistance the journalist might be able to offer. Luzadder agreed to meet with him. He wasn't sure what he could do to help the man, but it was a few days before Christmas and a notoriously slow time for breaking news. Who knew? Maybe the individual would offer up something worthwhile.

After checking in at the front desk, Luzadder was directed to a small, paint-chipped room on the third floor where he waited for his informant to arrive. When the inmate was brought in, the two exchanged pleasantries and cracked a few jokes before getting down to business. Luzadder gingerly broached the subject of the tip, and when the man leaned forward, he dropped a bombshell that would lead to a two-year odyssey and, quite possibly, a career-making story.

"Maybe," he said, "you'd like to know who killed the kids at the Burger Chef restaurant."

Luzadder was intrigued but cautious. In the six years since the Burger Chef murders, the case had moved beyond an unsolved mystery and had achieved something of a D.B. Cooper–like mythical status in the Circle City.

In 1982, Hardee's bought out the Burger Chef restaurant chain, and the Crawfordsville store was converted to the style of this New Albany Hardee's, circa 1983. *Courtesy of Kyle Brown's Burger Chef Memories website.*

Though the General Foods Corporation had sold Burger Chef to Hardee's Food Systems in 1982 for a reported $44 million, it remained an iconic brand locally, thanks in part to the infamous 1978 murders. Luzadder knew there had been numerous leads and several promising suspects but nothing that led to an arrest or conviction of the guilty parties. There had also been no closure for the families of the victims and the authorities who had worked the case for so long. Perhaps a combination of those factors compelled Luzadder to return to the jail a few weeks later to record the inmate's tale. As the informant laid out his facts, Luzadder said it was the kind of story that should have been easy to discount if it had no merit, but he couldn't.

"Something about it stuck. Something about it sounded right. Something about it could not be shaken," he said.

The inmate offered up a long monologue that contained no surprise twist or shocking revelations about the case, and it included few details about the crime. However, the man identified two individuals he believed to be responsible for the quadruple homicide. The first was a man detectives had already dismissed as a possible suspect, but the other was a former New Whiteland resident whom the inmate had known since he was a child. His name was Donald Ray Forrester.

WHO IS DONALD RAY FORRESTER?

Born on September 6, 1951, to Betty (née Ray) and Donald Forrester of New Whiteland, Donald Ray Forrester was a man who found himself on the wrong side of the law fairly early on in life. At the age of eighteen, he was arrested outside of The Scene youth center in downtown Franklin for disorderly conduct and public intoxication, and within months after that incident, he had warrants from the Marion County authorities for conducting a speed race, as well as from the Speedway Police Department for reckless driving. By July 15, 1969, the Franklin resident was being held in the Greenwood City Jail on a $3,000 bond for assault and battery with the intent to gratify sexual desires.

In 1977, Forrester's troubles continued. While serving a one-to-ten-year term for sodomy at the Indiana State Reformatory, he and fellow inmate Everett Decker got in trouble for holding prison counselor Morris Hammelman hostage at knife point. Forrester and Hammelman had been feuding for months ever since Hammelman gave Forrester a bad work report that resulted in a pay cut and less credit toward his time served. As their problems escalated, Hammelman suspended Forrester from his role as prison council president and refused to honor a request Forrester had made. That was the final straw as far as Forrester was concerned, and that was the moment when he and Decker took action. The standoff lasted two hours, and the pair surrendered only after speaking with reformatory superintendent George E. Phend.

Forrester served his time and was eventually released; however, he was not out of jail for long. On April 1, 1979, twenty-nine-year-old Forrester and his associate Ronald Dawson, eighteen, were arrested at a tavern near Castleton for the abduction and rape of a Hamilton County woman. According to the police report, the woman visited a Castleton nightclub that evening. Later in Noblesville, Forrester and Dawson approached her and forced her to get into their car at gunpoint. The pair drove the woman to Anderson, where they violated her before she was finally able to make her escape by jumping from the vehicle. Forrester was convicted of the crime and sentenced to ninety-five years in prison.

By the time his name was floated to Luzadder in connection with the Burger Chef case, Forrester was already well known to reporters at the *Indianapolis Star*. He'd contacted journalists in 1984 to encourage them to look into his October 4, 1983 escape attempt in which a sheriff's deputy fatally wounded a fellow inmate.

The incident occurred at Wishard Hospital, where Forrester and eight other inmates were taken to receive orthopedic treatment. Upon the inmates' discharge, officers were in the process of transferring Forrester, thirty-three; David Molnar, twenty-two; and Sylvester Brown, forty-seven, to a Department of Corrections van when the prisoners broke free of their restraints and made a break for it. Marion County sheriff's deputies and ambulance personnel were able to recapture Forrester and Molnar fairly quickly, but Brown bolted from the hospital loading area on 10th Street and failed to stop when Deputy Chris Cloud yelled for him to halt. Cloud fired one warning shot into the air, and when Brown continued to flee, he fired again—this time striking Brown in the back. Brown died of his injuries three hours later.

The Department of Corrections investigated the matter and concluded that Cloud acted appropriately in the situation, but Forrester disagreed and reached out to the *Star* in hopes that the paper could right what he perceived to be an injustice. After reading his impassioned letter, reporters thought it might be worth looking into, and they made arrangements to meet with Forrester in order to interview him about alleged prison abuses as well as the shooting of Brown.

The first time journalists came face to face with Forrester was in a stark meeting room at the Indiana State Reformatory. When guards brought Forrester in, he was shackled in handcuffs that were secured by a chain

The Pendleton Reformatory, where Donald Ray Forrester was a prisoner in 1984. Forrester would eventually confess being involved in the murder, but convicting him of the crime would prove difficult for authorities. *Author's private collection.*

THE BURGER CHEF MURDERS IN INDIANA

around his waist. Reporters had seen convicts before but no one quite like Forrester. His eyes had the haunted look of someone who spent too much time alone in solitary confinement and was resigned to his fate. He knew that he would spend the rest of his life behind bars and said he found it hard to get out of bed on some days. He explained that he'd found religion while in prison and was committed to helping others even if he couldn't help himself. He agreed to cooperate with reporters on their story investigating the internal abuses and the subsequent death of Brown.

Eight months later, a reporter for the *Indianapolis Star* returned to the reformatory, but this time Luzadder wanted to discuss a very different case.

DID YOU DO IT?

Before meeting with Forrester, Luzadder took the time to comb through the *Star*'s thick file on the Burger Chef murder mystery. He spent hours reading through articles, taking notes and speaking to the various reporters who had covered the incident since 1978, as well as Indiana State Police detective Donovan Lindsay, who, in 1985, was the only investigator still assigned to the case. Lindsay told Luzadder that the Burger Chef murders had become something of an obsession for him. He had a son who was roughly the same age that Daniel Davis had been at the time of his murder, and not only did Lindsay feel as though he knew each of the victims personally, but it bothered him that that no one had been brought to justice for the crime.

Lindsay told Luzadder that he was not surprised to hear Forrester's name in connection with the case. He was among the dozens of leads who were proffered in the early stages of the investigation but had not gone anywhere. Convinced that he may have information about the case, detectives offered him a reprieve on his ninety-five-year sentence if he came clean, but Forrester refused to cooperate.

"He did take two lie detector tests for us and failed them in part," Lindsay said. "We've always believed he knows something about the crime, but we are not sure what. He won't talk to us anymore."

Luzzader also learned that Forrester's ex-wife told authorities in 1979 that she accompanied her then husband to a place near the murder site in Johnson County a few weeks after the incident occurred. She said Forrester was looking for shell casings along a street near Stones Crossing Road, and after finding six, he took them home, flushed them down the toilet and made a phone call. Lindsay assured Luzadder that an interview with Forrester would not impede the ongoing investigation and he was interested in what the inmate might have to say on the subject. In the meantime, Lindsay gathered detectives Mel Willsey and Major Paul Simons to meet with Luzadder's original informant at the Marion County Jail to find out what else he might know about the Burger Chef murders.

On June 24, 1985, Luzadder met with Forrester. He looked more relaxed than he had when reporters visited him in the past. He was no longer bound and chained—a signal that his stint in solitary confinement was over. He asked Luzadder about the investigation into abuse allegations, and the journalist told him that requests for information from higher offices had been unsuccessful. A few other topics were touched on, and then, during a lull in the conversation, Luzadder broached the subject he came to discuss.

"The *Star* is making inquiries into the Burger Chef murders," Luzadder said. "And your name has come up."

Forrester leaned back in his chair, smiled and nodded but did not speak.

"Did you do it?" Luzadder pressed.

"No, I didn't," Forrester said simply.

An uncomfortable silence followed as Luzadder considered his options. He knew one wrong move might cause Forrester to shut down and say nothing else about the case. He mused aloud how hard it must have been for the four families to lose their children in such a horrific way and not have any answers.

"What no one can understand is why, why it happened," Luzadder finished.

Another uncomfortable silence followed.

"It was drugs," Forrester said at last. "Drugs and homosexuality."

Although Forrester maintained his innocence as far as the killings were concerned, he told Luzadder that he knew who did it and that he helped hide some evidence after the fact. He said there were at least two people involved, but he refused to divulge their identities out of fear that they might hear about it and retaliate against him or his family members. Forrester then pivoted to his own sentence, emphatically denying the rape charges that landed him in prison for ninety-five years and going into a long, rambling monologue about the contradictions in testimony by witnesses in the case, as well as the recanted testimony by his supposed accomplice.

Luzadder sensed an opening. He asked Forrester if he were to get him some help on his own conviction, would he be willing to tell authorities who was responsible for the Burger Chef murders?

"Yes," Forrester said. If it helped him get a new trial, then he would tell the reporter who was responsible for the quadruple homicide. He refused to tell the authorities, but he would tell Luzadder. "You just investigate it yourself. You'll find the answer."

Luzadder swung into action. Over the next two days, he launched a review of Forrester's conviction that thrilled Dr. Reece Townsend, DDS, and attorney Steve Sherman—two men who were involved in a local prison ministry and had taken an interest in Forrester's case. Both pored over thick files and transcripts looking for any loophole that might secure a new trial for their inmate, and they were excited to learn about the *Star*'s interest in Forrester as well.

"Praise the Lord," Townsend said. "I believe the Lord has plans for Don Forrester. He's made a dramatic turnaround in his life. He's a Christian now."

A week later, Luzadder received a call from Lindsay requesting a meeting at a downtown restaurant. Luzadder agreed, and when Lindsay arrived, he had Willsey and Simons with him. Acting on the 1979 tip from Forrester's ex-wife, the pair went to Forrester's former residence on the city's west side and opened up the septic tank. They found three shell casings, which backed up the original story.

Luzadder was stunned. After nearly seven years, it looked as though there may finally be a break in the Burger Chef case. However, cracking it wide open was another story. Lindsay said that information about the incident was becoming increasingly difficult to get ahold of. He didn't like the direction that the Marion County sheriff's detectives had taken on the investigation, and he doubted that Forrester would be willing to speak with them at all. What they really needed, he explained, was a mediator to help authorities communicate with Forrester. It needed to be someone with whom Forrester had established a rapport. It needed to be someone Forrester felt he could trust. It needed to be someone not connected to law enforcement.

Luzadder agreed to do it.

"DO THE RIGHT THING"

In July, investigators told Luzadder that the family of Forrester's ex-wife offered up the name of another individual who may have been involved in the murders. Luzadder agreed to pass the name along to Forrester in hopes that he might confirm or deny their participation, but before he could contact the reformatory and arrange a visit, the journalist received a short, handwritten letter from Forrester requesting a meeting. He wanted to talk about the Burger Chef murders, he said.

Luzadder wasted no time in getting into his car and driving the forty miles to the reformatory to meet with Forrester. To give the men a private place to chat, officials led Luzadder to an empty parole hearing office and brought Forrester in a few minutes later. He took a seat at the long conference table and apologized for the inconvenience but said that he no longer wanted to talk. As disappointment crossed Luzadder's face, Forrester assured him that when he wrote the letter, he genuinely wanted to discuss the case. However, after sitting with that decision over the weekend, he thought better of it. He was sorry, but he'd changed his mind.

Luzadder was frustrated. He did not drive all the way out to the reformatory only to be turned away. He was determined to try and salvage the conversation. He told Forrester that Marion County detectives were eager to speak with him, but Forrester refused to consider an official interview.

"No way," he cut in. "There were just some officers up here a few weeks ago. They told me why didn't I make them all heroes and tell them what they want to know. I told them to go to hell."

Luzadder thought fast and told Forrester that the authorities were mounting a case against him. "They have found some evidence. There's an informant who named you."

Forrester scoffed at the warning, saying the informant was probably lying in order to get out of trouble; there was no way anyone had any damning information on him. But Luzadder assured the inmate that it was not simply a scare tactic in order to get Forrester to cooperate.

"They have the shell casings," Luzadder went on. "They found them in the septic tank. They have a witness."

Forrester went pale and began to tremble. It was clear that Luzadder's words struck a chord even as he tried to cover. "How could they have a witness to something I didn't do?" he wanted to know.

Forrester surmised that the witness was probably an individual who knew just enough about the case to put the blame on him but who didn't really know all of the facts. He vacillated between trying to guess the name of the witness and insisting that he hadn't killed anyone. "I fired a shot over a guy's head once, but I never tried to kill anybody. Never," he said.

Luzadder sensed Forrester might crack, so he mentioned the shells again and told Forrester that it wouldn't be long before the detectives paid him a visit in order to get some information out of him. He said investigators had another name in connection with the crime, and when Forrester asked who it was, the reporter gave him the name supplied by his ex-wife.

Forrester's face sank. "That's it," he said. "That's him. They know who it is. As soon as they arrest him and the other one, they'll know it was me who talked."

Forrester explained that in the weeks after the murders, he was with a man who confessed his involvement in the crime. The man was under the influence of Demerol at the time, prompting Forrester to tell him to go to sleep, forget about it and never mention it again. It was now obvious that the advice had gone unheeded. Luzadder asked again if he might be willing to talk to detectives who were working on the case, but Forrester steadfastly refused.

On July 25, investigators arrived at the reformatory in hopes that Forrester had changed his mind about cooperating, but the prisoner remained resolute. In subsequent meetings, both Luzadder and Dr. Townsend urged Forrester to do the right thing and cooperate with the authorities for the sake of the victims and their families.

"It's what the Lord would want you to do," Townsend said.

Reluctantly, Forrester agreed, but he had to get something in return.

Chapter 10

A CONFESSION AT LAST?

On August 7, 1985, Marion County sheriff's detectives Mel Willsey and Paul Simons drove out to the Indiana State Reformatory to pick up Donald Ray Forrester. They had a court order as well as a letter from Marion County prosecutor Stephen Goldsmith promising the inmate limited immunity in exchange for his cooperation in the Burger Chef case. The plan was to drive Forrester out to Speedway in hopes that he could point out the place where he'd lived briefly between October 1978 and April 1979. The detectives believed that Forrester buried a burlap bag somewhere on the property that might contain bloodied boots, a coat, a murder weapon or other evidence pertaining to the case, and they needed his help to locate it.

Unfortunately, as investigators drove Forrester through his old neighborhood, the convict was unsure as to which house might have been his. All of the houses looked the same after so many years, and he didn't want to point out the wrong one. After driving around for several hours with no luck, the detectives decided to change tactics. They drove south to Johnson County, where Forrester had no trouble locating the spot where he'd picked up the shell casings a week after the murders. Encouraged, Willsey and Simons returned to Speedway, where Forrester continued to have difficulty identifying his former home.

"I'm not going to say a place is it if I'm not sure," Forrester told the exasperated officers. "I'm trying my best."

After several days of cruising through neighborhoods, Forrester tentatively pointed to a property on Patricia Street that looked familiar to him. He recognized the carport, fence line and a nearby school and felt it must be the place where he buried the evidence. Investigators did some quick research and were thrilled to discover that the owner was a man who worked with the other suspect named in the case. The following day, Donovan Lindsay, Willsey and Simons returned to the property with shovels and metal detectors in hopes of finding something incriminating. They dug for hours but uncovered nothing except dirt.

Convinced that Forrester chose the wrong property and was marred by incomplete recollections common with the passage of time, detectives transported Forrester to Akron, Ohio, to meet with a hypnotherapist who would try to help jog his memory. They hoped he might be able to come up with a few more details about his Speedway home, and when they returned, it appeared to have worked. Forrester had no trouble identifying the house he believed to be his former residence. Once again, authorities began to dig, and once again they found nothing.

Forrester was not a bit surprised that his burlap bag was no longer hidden on the property. He said the suspect was the kind of person who was always burying and reburying evidence, money, weapons and other important items, but investigators did not know what to believe. They were more than a little exasperated with the wild goose chase they appeared to be on, and they were beginning to doubt Forrester's credibility. Maybe he wasn't a reliable source after all.

"One day I think it's all lies and that he [Forrester] did it. The next I think he's telling the truth," Willsey said. "Mostly I think he is holding something back."

SHIELDING THE SOURCE

When all attempts to find buried evidence failed to produce results, investigators went back to square one: examining the known facts about the case and looking for any tidbit of information that might help them develop intelligence on the suspects Forrester named. They enlisted the help of Gary Maxey, a narcotics officer with the Marion County Sheriff's Department, and detective Robert Yarnell and tried to make contact with former girlfriends, co-workers or other associates who might know about any curious incidents that occurred in November 1978. They conducted a stakeout at one of the suspects' homes and gathered intelligence on a possible third suspect as well as a fourth.

It was a slow-moving process that was marred in part by the long-standing turf struggles between state and county officials, as well as the desire to shield their source from those who might learn of his cooperation and threaten his safety or the safety of his family.

Forrester was adamant that he would be labeled a snitch the moment he was removed from the reformatory unless authorities came up with a plausible cover story. Under the guise that there were new developments in his 1979 rape case, Forrester was moved to the Hamilton County Jail. However, he wasn't there very long before he began having health issues that resulted in multiple trips to the hospital and expensive medical bills. He became enough of a burden that the Hamilton County officials asked the state police to find other accommodations for him. Over the next several months, Forrester was held in the lock-up unit at the City-County Building in downtown Indianapolis and the Marion County Jail before doing another stint in Hamilton County. As the case proceeded at a snail's pace, even Forrester became frustrated and impatient with the lack of progress.

"I've given them what I know. They've got enough now to make some arrests. If they would talk to the people I told them to, they would get this done," he said.

For Forrester, a resolution in the Burger Chef case could mean a new trial for him, a shorter sentence or maybe even freedom, so he was just as anxious as the detectives were to see it end. But unfortunately, the new investigation ground to a standstill. After nearly a year since the *Star*'s Dan Luzadder first met with Forrester to discuss the Burger Chef murders, authorities were no closer to solving the case.

There was some good news at the start of 1986 when two new informants came forward. One of them named a suspect, independent of Forrester's lead, who might know something about the murders, while the other claimed to have seen this same individual accost Mark Flemmonds on the night of the murders. This was the same person who had worked with the state police in the past but whose relationship with authorities broke down after he refused to cooperate further. As he renewed his relationship with the current investigators, he provided some details that aligned with Forrester's narrative while others contradicted some of the established facts of the case. Detectives were not sure what to make of the discrepancy.

By the time summer rolled around, Forrester had caused enough trouble at the various correction facilities that he was transferred to the Indiana State Farm in Putnamville, where he was threatened by inmates and denied visits, showers and other privileges. Authorities were incensed that he'd been relocated when they still needed his help to crack their case, and they knew that exposing Forrester to violent inmates who thought him a traitor could have dire consequences for him. It was a fact Forrester knew as well.

"Knowing what I know about the prisons is enough to get me killed," Forrester said.

He wasn't killed, but he was tormented enough that two investigative reporters reached out to Goldsmith and asked him why he had Forrester moved.

"To my knowledge, Forrester hasn't given us a thing," the prosecutor said. "He's just taking a vacation from prison. What I'm told is that he hasn't helped the county at all. We think he's made this all up."

But what about the shell casings in his former home that were believed to be connected to the crime? Didn't that count for anything? Didn't the state have a duty to protect its informants? "What good would Forrester be…if he gets killed?" the reporters wanted to know.

"I wasn't ever told about that," Goldsmith admitted, vowing to look into the matter.

FORRESTER'S STORY FALLS APART

A year after Forrester was removed from the reformatory, investigators at the direction of Goldsmith arranged for Forrester to place a call to his prime suspect. They hoped that the individual would implicate himself during the conversation, which they planned to record and use against him in a court of law.

It was a last-ditch effort to get something useful out of Forrester before throwing in the towel. Unfortunately, the call did not go as well as they planned. They used a small tape recorder to capture the call, and for the most part, the quality was insufficient for their documentation purposes. They were able to salvage an exchange in which Forrester told the suspect that he planned to talk about the Burger Chef murders with the authorities unless the man gave him some money to hire an attorney. The suspect's response to the proposition raised questions among the investigators and gave them reason to believe they could solve the mystery at long last.

During their recent interviews with the other informants, detectives learned that the suspect's home on 17th Street had been linked to drug trafficking in the Speedway area and that Burger Chef assistant manager Jayne Friedt had been to the home on several occasions. So had her brother James, who was arrested on cocaine charges in 1981. Between this information and the taped conversation, it was enough smoke to convince Goldsmith there may be a fire. He agreed to return Forrester to the Marion County Jail.

But after receiving the call from Forrester, the suspect swung into action. He contacted members of Forrester's family in order to find out if the inmate had been released from prison. He called the state police to tell them that he was being blackmailed—unaware that they were part of the ruse. He submitted to an interview with the authorities, volunteered to take a lie detector test—which he passed—and told police that although he had nothing to do with the Burger Chef murders, he believed Forrester was involved. He pledged to do whatever was necessary to bring him to justice for the crime.

Police also met with the second individual named by Forrester, a longtime friend of the primary suspect, who also denied any involvement in the case. He, too, volunteered to take a polygraph test in order to prove his innocence, and when he passed, investigators realized the only guilty party appeared to be Forrester himself.

They just had to get him to admit it.

"You Are One of the Killers"

By the time detectives learned the result of the final polygraph on October 22, Forrester had been housed in an observation cell at the Marion County Jail for two months. He had a laundry list of complaints about his accommodations and was not shy about making his objections known. He said he was not allowed to have access to books or magazines and was denied his recreation time. A light someone left burning twenty-four hours a day bothered him. He claimed his food was tampered with, and he said guards told other inmates that he'd been diagnosed with AIDS (thus accounting for his placement in an observation unit).

Detectives assured Forrester that his safety was a primary concern, and for a while, they tried to placate him by arranging phone calls and allowing him some individual recreation time. But now, they were done playing. Detectives Maxey and Willsey called Forrester into an interrogation room and began grilling him while *Indianapolis Star* reporter Dan Luzadder looked on.

The detectives told Forrester that they spoke to the second suspect he named and learned that he'd been in the hospital on the night the murders occurred, which meant he could not have been involved in the crime. They accused Forrester of lying to them, withholding information and wasting their time.

"Your story isn't adding up anymore, Don," Willsey said.

Forrester became very quiet and asked the investigators to leave. He wanted to talk to Luzadder alone. The detectives hesitated and then reluctantly exited the room. When they were alone, Forrester leaned forward and began to cry. He told the reporter that he hadn't told police everything he knew about the Burger Chef case.

"I knew it was going to happen beforehand," he said.

Although his story remained more or less the same, he admitted to being present at a meeting that occurred three days before the murders took place. It was during this meeting that one of the suspects he named and several other men planned a visit to the restaurant in order to collect money for a drug debt.

Luzadder asked if the debt belonged to one of the men at the meeting, but Forrester shook his head. He said it belonged to Jayne. The men decided to confront Jayne about the debt, and if the money could not be collected at the time, then someone was going to pay up "one way or another." When the men approached Jayne at the restaurant, Mark Flemmonds intervened, and a scuffle ensued behind the restaurant. During the assault, Mark fell, hitting his head on the bumper of their van. Worried he had died from his injuries, they decided to eliminate the other witnesses. They abducted all of the crew members and drove them to the Johnson County woods where their bodies were found two days later.

Forrester repeated his new version of events to the detectives who said they suspected he'd been holding back. They were encouraged when Forrester insisted that the primary suspect he named was involved in the crime despite having been cleared by the lie detector test and that a new name surfaced that dovetailed with information they received from another source.

"This could be our real break," Willsey said.

But just as it appeared the case was coming together at last, investigators hit another snag. Police learned that one of the men named by Forrester was in federal prison at the time the alleged meeting took place. The detectives were furious that Forrester had lied once again, and they threatened to send him back to the reformatory immediately, regardless of his involvement in the Burger Chef case.

"You've either made up this entire story or you are one of the killers," they told him.

On Monday, November 10, 1986, investigators received a message from Forrester. He was ready to come clean at last. Maxey and Willsey went to his cell, and when they arrived, Forrester began to offer up detailed information about the case that could only be known by someone who was there. He outlined the positions of the bodies and the way they were configured at the murder scene. He described the individual wounds that were inflicted on the victims. He identified at least three other people who were involved in the crime. He even told police that the gun used in the murders was later thrown into the White River.

And he admitted that he was the person who shot Ruth Ellen Shelton and Daniel Davis.

Chapter 11

FORRESTER RECANTS

A week after confessing to two of the four murders in the Burger Chef case, Donald Ray Forrester recanted his statement, saying that authorities coerced him into making it. The thirty-six-year-old convicted rapist said he only confessed after investigators told him that they planned to send him back to the reformatory, where those who knew he'd cooperated with the police would threaten his life as well as the lives of his family members.

"I seen it coming that they would actually send me back [to the reformatory] to get killed," he said. "Not only me but my mother's life was in danger. They thought that was a funny joke."

Forrester insisted that he told investigators the truth when he said he attended a meeting with the real killers three days before the Burger Chef employees were abducted. He also acknowledged that he helped hide evidence after the fact, but he did not participate in the actual crime. He said any of the detailed information he gave authorities about the murders came from published reports about the case rather than any firsthand knowledge. In addition to recanting his own story, Forrester also cleared one of the suspects he'd previously named.

"I could not send an innocent man to prison," he said.

Authorities denied Forrester's allegation that they had strong-armed him into making a confession, but they were not surprised to hear that he had a change of heart. However, they remained skeptical of his claim that he was not involved somehow. He knew too much about the events of November 17, 1978, to be nothing more than an innocent bystander. He'd drawn a diagram of the Johnson County woods where the victims were found. He knew the positions in which the bodies were lying and the number of wounds each crew member sustained. He also claimed to have pulled the trigger that ended the lives of Ruth Ellen Shelton and Daniel Davis. Who would admit to something like that if they were not one of the guilty parties?

A crazy person would, and over the years, there have been more than a few people willing to take credit for the crime. Most were mentally unstable individuals or those eager to attach themselves to the infamy of the case, but they weren't privy to the information only the cops or the killers had. Forrester was, and authorities were confident that Forrester was not just another nutcase looking for his fifteen minutes of fame. They would not have gone to the trouble of moving him from the reformatory in order to enlist his help if they thought he was a liar. Police weren't surprised by Forrester's retraction, but they were puzzled by it.

"We had him out today, he was helping us. Everything was fine," said Major Paul Simons, chief investigator of the Marion County Sheriff's Department. "He took us to show us where he threw the gun in the river and where he threw the other weapon in Sugar Creek in Johnson County."

It was definitely an odd turn of events. Forrester told investigators that the gun used to kill Ruth Ellen and Daniel was stolen from a suburban area outside Marion County and after being used in the murders it was thrown into the White River from a bridge near downtown Indianapolis. Police immediately began formulating a plan to drag the river in search of the firearm, and they also organized underwater dives, but they knew it would be difficult to locate the gun due to changes in the river over the past eight years. Construction had disrupted the silt, and it was highly unlikely that even a powerful magnet could bring the weapon to the surface. Sugar Creek was dredged as well for the knife blade that was used to kill Jayne Friedt, but none of the searches turned up anything other than mud, muck and wet sand.

With Forrester recanting his confession and the lack of physical evidence, investigators needed to solidify their case against Forrester if they hoped to bring him to trial and secure a conviction in a court of law. They needed something that could connect him to the scene of the crime. Their research led them to review a seventeen-year-old molestation case involving Forrester that was all but forgotten to everyone but the victim and could prove that he had ties to the Burger Chef murder site long before the four crew members were found there.

The bridge near downtown Indianapolis where Donald Ray Forrester claimed to have tossed the gun that killed Ruth Ellen Shelton and Daniel Davis. *Courtesy of Vincent Johnson.*

AN ALL-BUT-FORGOTTEN CASE

On May 30, 1969, eighteen-year-old Forrester went for a Memorial Day weekend drive accompanied by a buddy and the buddy's girlfriend. While out and about enjoying the unofficial start-of-summer day, the trio stopped to pick up a fourteen-year-old girl who was acquainted with the couple but unfamiliar to the dark-haired man behind the wheel. The foursome drove around randomly for most of the afternoon, but at some point, Forrester pulled over and the couple exited the vehicle, leaving the young teenager alone with a man she'd just met. The girl assumed Forrester would take her home next, but when he drove by her house without stopping, she suspected that she was in danger.

Forrester took the teen to a secluded area off Stones Crossing Road near Van's Archery Shop, about a mile and a half from the Burger Chef murder site. There he sexually assaulted her in a "rude, insolent and angry manner." When he was finished, he returned her to her New Whiteland home.

The victim told her parents about the incident right away, and her father immediately reported it to the authorities. A warrant was issued, and Forrester was arrested on charges of intent to satisfy sexual desires and assault and battery. He was held on a $3,000 bond at the Johnson County Jail.

It was a charge that should have put Forrester away for up to five years due to the age of the victim; however, he never served a day for the crime. The following month, Forrester's attorney entered a not guilty plea on his behalf and requested a speedy trial as well as a reduced bond. Judge Robert Smith at the Johnson County Superior Court granted the request, and Forrester was released from prison the same day. After two continuances, Forrester pleaded guilty to the lesser charge of assault and battery. He was given six months' probation and a one-dollar fine and ordered to pay all court costs within thirty days.

When Forrester failed to pay his fine and court costs within the allotted time, Johnson County prosecutor Joe Van Valer filed a petition asking Judge Smith to revoke Forrester's probation. Smith set a hearing date, which Forrester failed to attend. A warrant was issued to the Marion County Sheriff's Department, but it was returned shortly afterward when they could not locate Forrester at his last known address. A few more motions were filed in the case, but then the paper trail petered out. Ultimately, the records were destroyed, and when Corporal Gary Maxey of the Marion County Sheriff's Department began looking into the case, he could not find any New Whiteland police officer that remember the incident.

"We couldn't make heads or tails out of it and the problem was that most of the records were expunged because the victim was a juvenile," Maxey said.

The only thing that might help harden their case against Forrester for the Burger Chef murders was if one of the other suspects he named corroborated the events he reported. Detectives spoke with some of the others Forrester pinpointed as having been involved in the crime. The first one was an individual whom police believed to be responsible for the stabbing death of Jayne Friedt. The suspect, who was already incarcerated in the Marion County Jail on an unspecified charge, denied participating in the murders, but he was initially willing to answer the detectives' questions about the case. A few days later, he stopped cooperating and said he would no longer talk to anyone without an attorney present.

A second suspect, who was named by Forrester more than a year before, was the leader of a drug ring based in the Speedway and Avon area that had been active at the time of the murders. While he willingly admitted to selling

Quaaludes, marijuana and various hallucinogens, he denied trafficking heavier drugs such as cocaine. He also denied any involvement in the Burger Chef murders. He was so adamant about his innocence that he called the *Indianapolis Star* and offered to submit to a polygraph and a "truth serum" test in order to prove it and prevent his name from being published.

"I didn't do it. I know it looks bad, but all the facts aren't known," he said.

The newspaper did not accept his offer and declined to publish his name on the grounds that he was not formally charged in the crime.

"We Are Standing on the Confession"

Despite a lack of substantive evidence, authorities remained confident that they had at least one of the parties responsible for the Burger Chef murders, and on November 10, 1986, they asked Marion County prosecutor Stephen Goldsmith to bring charges against Forrester for his role in the horrific crime. They insisted not only that he was present when the murders were planned and executed, but they also believed that he fired the weapon that killed two of the victims.

"We are standing on the confession," Simmons said. "We'll ask Mr. Goldsmith to file formal charges against Forrester....If he decides against [filing the charges], I assume Forrester will return to prison."

Goldsmith was torn on the issue. On the one hand, it would be nice to finally charge someone in the crime that had eluded investigators for so long, but there was no guarantee that the charges would result in a conviction. Forrester's story had changed so much over the past two years that it was all but impossible to determine exactly what his role in the incident might have been. On the surface, it seemed obvious that he was, in fact, present at the scene of the murders and more than likely took part in them, but as far as who did what to whom, that was hard to determine, and it would be even harder to prove beyond a reasonable doubt.

Marion County chief trial deputy David Cook said there were a number of people in Goldsmith's office who were wary of working with Forrester from the very start. They were concerned that variations in his story were a plot to secure a reduced sentence in his rape case and that even if he were to stick to one version of events for any length of time, they still needed corroborating evidence such as a murder weapon or eyewitness testimony in order to convict him, and they didn't have it.

"If you have been exposed to him for a year and a half as I have, you believe that he was involved somehow—either by being there when the murders occurred or having actual knowledge of the people involved," he said.

Goldsmith also had concerns that Forrester's confession could have been influenced by published reports about the case. When James Friedt was arrested on a cocaine charge in 1981, he offered up a theory that it was his sister Jayne who was initially confronted by the murderers, but when Mark Flemmonds stepped in to intervene, things took a turn for the worst. This was the same scenario Forrester offered. Was it possible that he read James's hypothesis and adopted it as his own? Goldsmith ordered that a comparison be made between Forrester's statements and accounts that were published in the media to determine if one might have had an impact on the other. He said he would make a decision about the suspect by Christmas.

The families of the four victims felt little vindication after learning that Forrester might be charged with the murders of their loved ones. In fact, the news brought a fresh wave of grief and painful memories of the past. Robert Flemmonds said he occasionally drove by the restaurant where his son and three co-workers were last seen alive on November 17, 1978, but it was not easy to do so knowing that no one had paid for the crime.

"I always held out hope that someday the guilty parties would be apprehended," he said. "I don't hold a grudge, there's no revenge factor. I feel for them, really. It's the crime I hate."

John Shelton, father of Ruth Ellen, said he and his wife, Rachel, had mixed feelings about the latest break in the case. While they were pleased that someone might be held responsible for the death of their daughter at long last, the renewed interest in the case made it difficult to move on.

Every anniversary of Ruth Ellen's death was difficult, like the ache of a phantom limb, but this year it was like ripping open an old wound. "This time of year, we're tore up about it anyway," John said.

It wasn't only the families who were happy to see the baffling mystery possibly come finally to an end; Indiana State Police sergeant Leon Griffiths, who had been an investigator on the case until 1982, said he, too, never gave up hope that the murderer would be found.

"It's a thing I lived with for a long time….It was so intense. It comes up all the times when I'm talking to the other investigators. The parents of those kids will never put it to rest and I don't think it will ever leave my memory. Hopefully, maybe now, it will come to a successful conclusion," he said.

TIME RUNS OUT

While law enforcement officials, families and the rest of the community awaited Goldsmith's decision, Forrester sensed that his time was almost up. If Goldsmith did not charge him with the murders, he would be returned to the reformatory, and any chance of revisiting his rape conviction would be lost. In an effort to complicate matters and buy himself some additional time, Forrester told journalists that he hoped Goldsmith would charge him with the crime. Although he maintained that he'd been forced into making his confession, the only way to prove his innocence once and for all was to stand trial.

Journalists were unconvinced that authorities had mistreated Forrester while he was held at the Marion County Jail, but during his interview, he told them that he was drugged prior to his confession, which led to his admission of guilt. He denied that he'd ever pinpointed the exact location of the bodies on a map of Johnson County, and he claimed that he'd never waived his right to consult with an attorney despite his signature appearing on the document.

"I've never signed one of those in my life," he insisted.

Simons refuted Forrester's claim that he was drugged, saying that both blood and urine samples had been taken from the inmate at the time of his accusation and all of the lab reports came back negative. He scoffed at Forrester's next suggestion—that the samples were tampered with somehow—and said the whole thing was a ploy to confuse and distract the public.

"It's all a bunch of bull," Simons said.

On December 20, 1986, Goldsmith called a meeting with investigators and members of his own office to discuss the possibility of bringing Forrester to trial. With no evidence other than his word—his now recanted word—could they successfully prosecute the case?

Goldsmith's deputies were split on their opinions. Some felt strongly that they could bring Forrester to justice, while others expressed reservations about bringing the case to trial. Cook was among those hesitant to press charges. "He just told so many different versions that we didn't believe him. We have used every means available to us to weigh the credibility of the information he has to give and we are not convinced that what he says is correct....Someday it may be shown that Forrester was involved...[but] whether he was involved or not is up for grabs."

After reviewing Forrester's 1,200-page statement and discussing it with the primary parties involved, the prosecutor called a news conference and announced that he would not bring charges against Forrester for the Burger Chef murders.

Goldsmith stressed his decision was not to be taken as a vindication of Forrester or a reflection on the competence of the detectives involved. He believed the authorities were diligent in their efforts and that Forrester was still a suspect in the case, but he didn't feel they had enough to secure a guilty verdict. He promised to reexamine the matter should more evidence come to light, but at this time, Forrester would be returned to the state facility. The Burger Chef case would remain open, but it seemed highly unlikely that it would ever be solved.

"It's been eight years, and we haven't solved it yet. The longer it is, the more difficult the crime is to solve," he said.

Chapter 12

THE YEARS GO BY

W hen Marion County prosecutor Stephen Goldsmith opted not
to press charges against Donald Ray Forrester for his possible
role in the Burger Chef murders, authorities made plans to
transfer the convicted felon back to the Indiana State Reformatory. It was
easier said than done. Department of Corrections deputy commissioner
Cloid Shuler realized that returning Forrester to the state institution would be
problematic because he had violated the unwritten but understood "inmate
code" prohibiting prisoners from assisting law enforcement agencies.

The first step in safely transferring Forrester was to send him to the
Reception and Diagnostic Center in Plainfield, where behavioral specialists
could evaluate him before he was sent to the Indiana State Prison in
Michigan City.

"Our options are limited," Shuler said. "It's difficult to protect anyone
with such a high degree of visibility, especially in light of allegations made
in public about others."

A MILESTONE IS REACHED

On November 17, 1988, the Burger Chef murder mystery marked its ten-
year anniversary. To commemorate the occasion, *Indianapolis Star* reporter
Dan Luzadder caught up with Forrester at his new home, where he spent

each day working as a porter, serving meals and cleaning offices from 5:30 a.m. until lights out at 9:00 p.m.

Even behind bars, Forrester continued to feed information to others about the case. He maintained that he was merely an accessory to the crime and that he alone held the key to solving the mystery once and for all. But no one knew what to believe when it came to Forrester. He made rambling phone calls to Luzadder in which he reported hearing voices and said that prison officials were performing surgeries on him. He claimed that he'd been implanted with a device that controlled his thoughts and he was powerless to stop it.

In 1987, Forrester was sent to a psychiatric ward at the Westville Correctional Facility for refusing medical treatment. After several weeks, during which he claimed he was drugged against his will, he was returned to Michigan City, where he received a weekly dose of Thorazine for his mood disorder.

Forrester knew he would be in prison for the rest of his life, and as far as he was concerned, the end could not come soon enough. "The best thing I could do is die.…If you can't get out of prison, what's left?…For me, this is my own kind of Death Row. Only worse.…People have no idea what prison is like.…There is no justice in here. They could do something to help me, a time cut or something for helping.…But they don't want the truth. And they don't care about those kids either. They wanted the glory of solving the case, but they haven't done it yet, have they?"

He had a point. Over the course of the decade, the investigation took detectives to sixteen different states and brought in leads from as far away as West Germany. There were approximately twenty thousand names associated with the case, including informants, potential informants and possible suspects. Yet no one had been charged and convicted of the crime. The case remained open, and the $25,000 reward was still in place. There was even an investigator assigned to work on the case in his spare time, but according to Sergeant Gary Wilkinson, investigation coordinator with the Indiana State Police Department, new leads were few and far between. "Probably most of the leads we get are from convicts or ex-convicts, but other than that, there are no solid leads coming in," he said.

Because Forrester continued to talk about the case, it was not surprising that most of the ten-year tips came from the inmates at the Michigan City facility. However, detectives had become more discerning about the information they received either directly or indirectly from the only solid suspect they had in the case. They learned the hard way what happened

The state prison in Michigan City where Donald Ray Forrester was sent after prosecutors failed to bring a case against him in connection to the Burger Chef murders. *Author's private collection.*

when they let the desire to solve the case skew their perception where Forrester was concerned.

"There were people who wanted to solve the crime so bad that they weren't paying attention to the total picture of Donald Ray Forrester," said Marion County trial deputy David Cook. "They wanted to take it as absolute evidence when it was just another crazy thing he said."

BURYING THE PAST

Ten years after their children's lives were tragically cut short, the families of the Burger Chef crew members had moved on. Although there was not a day that went by in which they didn't think about their precious young people, they could not let the pain of the past take away from any future joy they might experience.

Rachel Shelton said time helped her heal and make peace with the death of her daughter Ruth Ellen. As a woman of deep faith, she gave all the negative emotions she felt to God and enlisted the support of a counselor who helped her talk through her feelings, confront the truth, acknowledge the pain and learn to live again. "You can't live in a little circle of something that you cannot change. Some people do, but if they do, then they end up being a vegetable," she said.

Like Rachel, Robert Flemmonds said he, too, relied on his faith to help him endure the nightmare of losing his son Mark. Over the past ten years, he leaned on the Old Testament story of King David, who prayed for God to spare the life of his son, but despite his petitions, the boy died anyway. "The boy passed. It was too late. That is the principle I try to live by. We lost our son in a tragic death, but we can't change that, so we have to get on with life," he said.

Once the case against Forrester fell apart in 1986, and with no other suspect in sight, neither parent felt confident that the mystery would ever be solved or that any of the killers would be caught, tried and convicted. And they no longer woke up every day waiting for the police to call with news.

"I can't," Shelton said. "I would be in terrible shape if I lived with that on my mind for ten years."

But even though she'd buried the past, she still hoped that one day, justice might still be served. "Part of you wants to see it come to trial, and part of you doesn't. If [the murderer] gets in the news again, I would get emotionally involved again, and I don't want to do that.…Yesterday's hurts are yesterday, and you don't want to hurt again," she said.

Flemmonds understood the mixed emotions Shelton felt in wanting to see the case resolved; however, he was less concerned with quelling his own pain than he was with putting an end to an expensive and time-consuming investigation. "It would stop the money being spent, and the police could go on to something else. I'm sorry that they have done all that work and can't find the answer," he said.

In 1993, Indiana State Police lieutenant Jim Cramer reflected on the case that had puzzled authorities for fifteen years. He was forty-two years old and the only original detective on the case who was still employed by the agency. He still did not know who might have been responsible for the deaths of the four crew members, but he was pretty sure that the murders were not premeditated.

"Based on what we know about what occurred in the woods, the way the people were killed and the instruments of death that were used, it doesn't seem logical to me that anyone went in [the restaurant] with the intention of killing anyone," he said. "I assume things got out of hand. Something occurred to trigger this."

The basic facts remained the same: investigators believed that the incident most likely started out as some kind of cash grab but then turned into something more serious when one of the crew members recognized one of the suspects. In an effort to eliminate any witnesses, the perpetrators abducted the employees using Jayne Friedt's car to help mask their getaway. After transferring the employees to a secondary vehicle and abandoning Jayne's Vega, the suspects drove to a wooded area of Johnson County, where they murdered the four employees in three distinct ways. The bodies were discovered two days later by a middle-aged couple who stumbled upon the crime scene while out for an afternoon walk.

However, Cramer said the police never conclusively established a motive for the crime, nor had they determined whether or not any of the employees did anything to precipitate their deaths. Unofficially, there were two camps: those who believed that the murders were carried out by a group of people who had a history of robbing fast-food restaurants in the area, including at least one Burger Chef in the summer of 1978; and those who believed that a group of men, including Donald Ray Forrester, went into the restaurant in order to collect money for a drug debt but were thwarted when someone unexpectedly recognized them. Either scenario was possible, but solving the crime was made infinitely more difficult with the mistakes that were made in the beginning, the bickering back and forth between agencies and the hasty decision to release the composite sketches of the two men who were seen behind the Burger Chef by two teenagers on November 17, 1978.

"In retrospect, it may have been wiser to not release those [sketches]—to wait for two weeks or a month. Then when we'd get the calls, we would have had these drawings to compare to," Cramer said.

Cramer was among those who interviewed Forrester several times while he was in prison, but he remained skeptical about what role—if any—Forrester played in the crime. In his opinion, the 1986 confession was little more than an attempt to get out of jail free or at the very least to secure a sentence modification. Either way, Forrester's admission didn't wash with him.

"He's never told me the first thing that was credible about this case," he said.

Cramer said out of the hundreds of tips authorities received over the years, only eight to twelve were truly promising. Most of the suspects were questioned and then quickly cleared, but those left behind were difficult to discount. Police could not prove conclusively that they were involved in the murders and they couldn't prove that they weren't.

"Only one person came forward who has information closely approaching being an eyewitness, a potential eyewitness or have knowledge of what occurred," he said.

That person was the individual who was in the Dunkin' Donuts on November 17, 1978, and could have seen what was happening at the Burger Chef next door. The individual eventually recanted his story, saying he was never in the donut shop on the night in question, but police have another witness who saw him there.

"He's either a liar—and I can prove he's not lying—a witness or one of the persons who committed the crime," Cramer said.

While Cramer never named the individual, it is believed to be a man who was stationed across the street from the Burger Chef and saw the four crew members being taken from the back door of the restaurant just prior to their deaths. He confirmed the presence of the man in the donut shop next door to the Burger Chef, but it is unclear what his role might have been. Cramer said he could be someone who had the opportunity to see what happened or could have been one of the people responsible for the murders. It was impossible to know for sure. "We can't prove that, or he would be in jail,"

Ken York always believed that robbery was the motive behind the Burger Chef murders. After twenty-five years as an Indiana State Police detective, York retired in 1992 and moved to Mesa, Arizona. However, the case continued to haunt him. He said there is always one case that stands out—the one that didn't get solved—and for him it is the Burger Chef case. He maintained that three Johnson County men were responsible for the killings, and he implored then Johnson County prosecutor Charles Gantz to convene a grand jury to investigate the circumstantial evidence, but Gantz did not feel there was enough proof to secure a conviction. There was simply no direct evidence that could link the men with the crime.

"I don't think there was ever enough to go to a grand jury," he said, noting that with so many leads in the case, it would be an all-but-impossible task for any prosecutor to eliminate all but three people. "This was never a case where it developed to the point where there were several suspects or one suspect and you could say, 'This is the guy who did it.'"

York acknowledged that a solid circumstantial case could be made against a couple of different groups of individuals but remained confident that he knew who was behind the murders.

"I'll go to my grave believing the group I worked on [was responsible]," he said. "[But] it would be extremely difficult—if not impossible—to convict them."

Gantz agreed with that assessment. "There's too much difference between a policeman's hunch, probable cause and a successful prosecution. You don't deal with hunches—you've got to have solid proof."

After spending the last decade and a half pursuing every lead available, wading through the quagmire of the Forrester confession and running into dead end after dead end, Cramer was pragmatic about the possibility of resolving the case once and for all. If they hadn't charged anyone yet, it was unlikely that they would. If the killers were not dead already or in jail for another offense, then they were probably walking free. It was as if they had committed the perfect crime—and had gotten away with murder.

GONE, BUT NOT FORGOTTEN

By 1998, the physical reminders of the Burger Chef murder mystery had faded and evolved with the passage of time. The Crawfordsville Road restaurant, assumed by Hardee's after the 1982 buyout, was closed and the building transformed into an auto parts store, appliance store and several other businesses before settling into an empty storefront. The twenty acres of Johnson County woods where the crew members' bodies were found were sold to a developer who cleared the land to make way for the Timber Heights subdivision. But for the families, the memories remained. The past was gone, but it was far from forgotten.

George and Carolyn Friedt said there were days when they thought that they had finally run out of grief. The couple moved to Hendricks County, and in the two decades since their daughter's death, there were days in which they could actually thank God for relieving them of their pain. Unfortunately, that relief was always short-lived. Someone would ask about Jayne. They would read about a new lead in the newspaper, or they would turn on the television and see footage of the police pulling Jayne's body out of the woods once again. "You thought you'd forgotten about it and they just keep bringing it up and bringing it up and bringing it up," Carolyn said.

The reality of what occurred was difficult to bear, and Carolyn said she would rather focus on the good times she had with her child: a trusting, open, loving, friendly person who always went out of her way to help others.

The former Heger property, where the bodies of the four Burger Chef crew members were found, is now a Johnson County subdivision called Timber Heights. *Author's private collection.*

She was grateful for those moments when the pain was unbearable, but she would never wish it on someone else. "I hope to God no one else ever has to go through this…and endure this kind of grief," she said.

Retired Indiana State Police detective Leon Griffith said he thought about the four young crew members frequently over the years and occasionally wept for their unfulfilled lives. He was thirty-eight when the murders occurred and was among the investigators assigned to the case. He endured eighteen-hour days, chased down hundreds of leads and examined the facts from so many angles that it literally made him sick. A few months after the murders, he was admitted to Community Hospital East for extreme exhaustion. Two decades later, he could still remember some of the most random facts and minor details of the case. "We never came up with anything concrete where we said, 'We believe these people were involved in this,'" he said.

Griffith was not the only officer to be personally affected by the murders. Buddy Ellwanger blamed the murders, in part, for the breakdown of his marriage. The long hours and the desire to track down the killers became his priority, and everything else was relegated to the back burner. The retired Speedway police officer said he was fairly confident his marriage was not the only one that succumbed to the case. "You kind of take it personally," he said. "You really do. You almost forget about your family and concentrate on that. It's the only thing on your mind. It takes over your life. It does."

Mayor Stephen Goldsmith, who was the Marion County prosecutor in 1979, said the Burger Chef murders were the kind of case that devastated the families of the victims, changed the lives of the officers involved and shattered the peace of an entire community. He said it was Indianapolis's jumping-off point into the violence that previously only happened in bigger cities. Although there had been a few spectacular murders in the past, the fact that this one involved four young adults working in a fast-food store made the city feel more vulnerable than it ever had before.

"It was huge," he said.

Chapter 13

OPEN BUT INACTIVE

Much has changed throughout central Indiana since the events of November 17, 1978, but one thing remains the same. To date, no one has been charged, tried or convicted in the murders of Jayne Friedt, Ruth Ellen Shelton, Daniel Davis and Mark Flemmonds. And it's unlikely that anyone ever will.

"At first, I was convinced that it would be solved," Rachel Shelton said in 2003. "I guess we sure don't hold our breaths about it. It was a long time ago."

While some of the families and individuals associated with the Burger Chef case distanced themselves geographically, the Sheltons continued to live in the same Speedway home where they raised their beloved Ruth Ellen along with their two younger children, Gordon and Theresa. Instead, they distanced themselves emotionally from the tragedy that could not bring their daughter back and would only serve to hurt rather than to heal. "I don't want to live with that every day. Life has to go on," Rachel said. "I don't want to live with the pain that I had then. That would be an unhealed [wound], and you can't be unhealed and still go on."

In a rare 2003 interview with the *Daily Journal* of Franklin, Rachel, then sixty-seven, had retired and was looking forward to starting her golden years when her husband, John, sixty-eight, retired from Allison Transmission later in the year. Their other two children were adults, and the family had learned to move on, but Rachel said she occasionally found herself reflecting on the life her oldest might have led had she not been denied her high school graduation, college education, career, marriage and family on a cold November night.

Ruth Ellen would have been forty-two that year and no doubt in the throes of a busy, happy life. For several years, Rachel said she mourned the children Ruth Ellen would never have, but she insisted that she learned to forgive those responsible for her daughter's death even if she couldn't forget what they did. "That's the only way to live," she said. "If I could still see them beating or mistreating my child, human nature would rise up; but the bottom line is to forgive."

John Shelton agreed that it was important to forgive his daughter's killers, but if they were caught, he wouldn't want to see them get away with the crime. Several years earlier, he said that the Indiana State Police told him that they more or less knew who carried out the crime, and when asked if he wanted to know their names, John politely declined. However, if anyone were charged, both he and Rachel would want those individuals prosecuted to the fullest extent of the law.

"I'm not standing wanting to leap on anybody for revenge, because all revenge is turned over to God," Rachel said. "I would love to know that whoever was involved, whoever did this, got right with God."

Carolyn Friedt was the only other Burger Chef family member to publicly commemorate the twenty-fifth anniversary of her daughter's death. The Davis family slipped from the spotlight shortly after Daniel's death, and Robert Flemmonds, who occasionally granted interviews about his son Mark, died on December 25, 1991. Flemmonds's wife, Blondell, was never comfortable giving statements to the press, which left Friedt to be the only other voice to speak on behalf of the victims' loved ones.

Carolyn said if the case were to be solved after twenty-five years, it would have to be a deathbed confession, but she eschewed milestone anniversary retrospectives because they caused fresh waves of pain for the families and a lot of unwanted attention from the media. "Every news story and TV report means we have to go through the pain of burying them again in our hearts," she said.

First Sergeant Bill Vann said he understood Carolyn's pain and irritation at having to revisit the murders. He was a teenager when the four young crew members were kidnapped and killed, but twenty-five years later, he was the parent of a daughter in high school and sensitive to the emotions the families must feel as each anniversary passed.

Vann inherited the case in 1998, and he was familiar with every wild theory, rumor and innuendo the families had been subjected to over the years. Although the case remained open, it was inactive with no new developments on the horizon. Vann said he still worked on the case in his spare time, and every eighteen months to two years, tips would trickle in, but the information included in those tips was rarely worth investigating.

Speedway police chief Jeff Dine refused to give up hope. Dine had been a dispatcher at the time of the murders and was the one who took the call from Brian Kring reporting the opened door and the missing employees at the restaurant. He said he hoped that case would be resolved at some point for the families' sake as well as the victims themselves. "Whether or not that happens remains to be seen. But the case was not put on a shelf and forgotten," he said.

Dine retired from the Speedway Police Department in July 2018.

Dignity for the Deceased

In 2008, the Burger Chef murders were in the news once again. The Department of Corrections announced that the case would be featured in a new set of playing cards that were sold to inmates at state facilities such as the one in Michigan City. It was hoped that the unsolved mysteries included on these "cold case" decks would help jog a latent memory and encourage an individual to come forward. However, the strategy did not lead to any new developments in the thirty-year-old case.

That same year, George Friedt, the father of slain Burger Chef assistant manager Jayne Friedt, died at the age of eighty-three. George had been a ticket taker and conductor for the New York Central, Penn-Central, Conrail and Amtrak railroads and was a member of the United Train Workers' Union and the Rusty Rails Association. His wife and three of Jayne's siblings survived him.

Mark Flemmonds's mother, Blondell, passed away three years later on February 5, 2011, at the age of seventy-six, followed by Carolyn Friedt on June 10, 2012, at the age of eighty, leaving Rachel Shelton as the last known surviving Burger Chef parent. Her husband, John, preceded her in death on May 8, 2005, and in preparation for the thirty-fifth anniversary of the murders, Rachel gave her final interview to WTHR-13. She died on November 8, 2013, just before the segment aired. "I have two children alive and one in heaven," she said.

The graves of George and Carolyn Friedt located in Roselawn Memorial Cemetery in Terre Haute. They are buried adjacent to their daughter Jayne and their son who died in infancy. *Author's private collection.*

The graves of John and Rachel Shelton located at Washington Park West in Indianapolis. The couple gave several interviews over the years regarding their daughter Ruth Ellen's promising life and tragic death. *Author's private collection.*

Rachel's surviving daughter, Theresa Jefferies, also appeared in the retrospective to talk about the sister she lost so long ago. She showed off the last dress her grandmother made for Ruth Ellen, which the teen wore in a family photo, as well as a high school ring featuring two intertwined hearts. While the keepsakes help to keep the memory of her sister close, she said she still has nightmares about the way Ruth Ellen and the others died, and she experiences periods of sadness when the weather grows cold each November.

Sergeant Vann was interviewed for the piece and maintained that the crime was committed by a group of five individuals who targeted local Burger Chefs for robbery, including Dave Cathcart, who initially bragged about his involvement in the crime back in 1978; John Defibaugh; and S.W. Wilkins. Vann said one of them was probably recognized by a crew member during the robbery, which prompted the suspects to commit murder. At first glance, it appeared to be the same old theory, but Vann suggested a slight twist to the known narrative. Vann believed it was possible that the reason one of the robbers and the employee knew each other is because he was a regular at another Burger Chef franchise where Jayne Friedt had previously worked. Sergeant Vann believed it was the bearded man who recognized the young assistant manager. "It would be nice to be able to confirm that relationship of recognition," he said. "It doesn't mean that it would solve the case, it just means that it would put another piece into the puzzle and one step closer."

Cathcart committed suicide within a decade of the murders, while Defibaugh was shot to death in 2004. Wilkins succumbed to a heart attack in 1993 at the age of thirty-four. The other two associates of the group are alive and remain residents of Indiana. A news crew tracked one of those surviving men to his home in October 2018 and was told that he passed two polygraph tests when questioned by the authorities. He also said there was no DNA evidence linking him to the scene of the crime. He continues to deny any personal involvement in the incident but refused to go on the record and clear his name once and for all. He also said he did not think the case would ever be solved.

Jefferies said she did not honestly believe that the case would ever be solved, but if anyone had any information that might help the authorities riddle out a few more of the facts, she wished they would come forward. "I would like to have whoever did this be not available to do it to others," she said.

With a case as well publicized and heavily covered as the Burger Chef murders, it is hard to believe that there could be any piece of information

The grave of Mark Flemmonds at the New Crown Cemetery in Indianapolis. For years, the teen's grave was unmarked, but thanks to a fundraiser led by a local radio host, a headstone was purchased and installed. *Author's private collection.*

concerning it that had not come to light over the past thirty-five years, but in 2015, that's exactly what happened. WNDE radio host Jake Query discovered that sixteen-year-old Burger Chef victim Mark Flemmonds was buried in an unmarked grave at the New Crown Cemetery located at 2101 Churchman Avenue in Indianapolis. He wanted to bring some dignity to Mark's burial site and launched a Twitter campaign to raise money to supply a headstone for the Speedway teen who was gone too soon.

Within fifteen minutes, more than $800 was raised, and by the time all the pledges were collected, enough money had come in to purchase an even nicer headstone than was initially planned. It was a tribute that touched Taylor Simonis, the manager of the New Crown Cemetery.

"People in our community, not just one person, multiple people, still feel that cemeteries are a good way to show and remember love for somebody," he said.

The stone reads: *Mark Flemmonds 1962–1978 beloved brother, son and friend. Speedway High School Class of 1981.*

"IT'S TIME"

Today, the library of information pertaining to the Burger Chef murder mystery is housed at the Indiana State Police Post 52 on East 21st Street. It includes more than two dozen three-ring binders of police notes; numerous reel-to-reel audio, video and cassette tapes of interviews; the original composite sketches; and the clay busts made of the primary suspects days after the murders occurred. The police also have the blood-soaked brown-and-orange uniforms the crew members were wearing when they died, along with the bullets extracted from Ruth Ellen and Daniel, the knife blade used to kill Jayne, the cigarette butts found in the ash tray of Jayne's white 1974 Chevrolet Vega and the car itself. In addition, they have hair and blood samples from each of the victims along with their fingerprints in the event there are advances in forensic technology or new evidence in the case comes to light.

In 2017, Bill Vann announced that he was retiring from the department after twenty-nine years of service. As he prepared to leave, he transferred his caseload to other detectives. He passed the Burger Chef case to Nicholas Alspach, a Johnson County native, Franklin College graduate and Iraq War veteran who joined the agency in 2007. Alspach had a special connection to the case. His grandfather Sherrill Alspach was the crime scene technician who processed Jayne's Vega and lifted the palmprint that led to a fringe friend of one of the victim's brothers in 2007. While the lead did not go anywhere, it was the most activity the case had in years and the last time Vann was excited about a possible lead.

The younger Alspach said he has no idea if he will be able to solve the cold case, but he continues to field calls regarding the event and is willing to see what he might be able to accomplish.

"Under no circumstances would you want to see this get colder, or any colder than it already has been over 39-plus years," he told WIBC radio. "Things like this [interview] are incredibly beneficial to bring it back into the public eye so that they can possibly bring forth something....It might just be a small piece that could bring something together."

Alspach said when a detective is handed a case of this magnitude, it is important to go back over everything to see if something, somewhere along the line might have been overlooked and if there are new technical applications available that might help shed some light on the dead ends to see if there might be a path forward. He is quick to point out there have been plenty of competent detectives on the case over the years and that it

Above: Today, the former Burger Chef on Crawfordsville Road in Speedway is an empty storefront, but over the years, it has been an auto parts store and a Cash$Land store. *Author's private collection.*

Left: The doorway from which four Burger Chef crew members were abducted on November 17, 1978, as it appears today. *Author's private collection.*

The back view of the former Burger Chef restaurant on Crawfordsville Road in Speedway, Indiana. *Author's private collection.*

was not for a lack of skill or effort that they were unable to crack it. While it is a daunting process, Alspach feels it is important to try to go back over everything with a fresh and unbiased eye, to put aside preconceived notions and popular theories about the case and see where the case leads him.

"Somewhere in that process, maybe we'll find a little bit more. Maybe the tech we have nowadays with DNA, maybe we'll have the ability to cross that threshold," he said. "We'll see where the case takes us."

Alspach ultimately passed the case on to Sergeant Bill Dalton, an eighteen-year veteran of the Indiana State Police who was only four years old when the crime occurred. Not only is he committed to resolving the case, but he is also working to digitize the existing files and employ the latest technologies on the evidence in hopes that the techniques will offer up new clues and leads.

In commemoration of the fortieth anniversary of the event, Dalton held a press conference to give the public an update on where the case stands. While the proceedings were primarily held to remind the community that the police have never given up on the crime for the first time, Dalton displayed a photo of one of the murder weapons: the knife blade that killed Jayne Friedt.

The blade was not part of a pocketknife but a four-and-a-half-inch hunting blade that was broken off at the handle and most likely carried in a sheath on the murderer's belt. Police hoped that by releasing the photo, it might help jog someone's memory who may recall knowing someone who wore something so distinctive. "I'm hoping this will generate some tips," Dalton said.

Theresa Jefferies sat alongside the detectives as they talked about the new technology and techniques they planned to use in order to resolve the case. She expressed confidence in the new investigative approaches and encouraged anyone holding onto a forty-year-old secret to come clean once and for all.

"These aren't just victims. That was my sister," she said. "Jayne, Mark, Daniel and Ruth are real people with real families and real friends that deserve justice. When there's a murder involved, it's harder to move on. We don't have the answers and there's someone out there who does....If you're sitting on a secret from 40 years ago, then you're sitting out of fear. That means you are a victim just as much as they were. It's time."

EPILOGUE

Over the last four decades, the Burger Chef murders have become one of the most infamous unsolved mysteries in the state of Indiana. Each year, print and broadcast media recount the events of November 17, 1978, and offer an update on where the case stands today. They reach out to family members, still grieving loved ones, detectives who were once part of the investigation and those who are still involved to talk about their experiences with the horrific crime. They remind the public that the case remains open and the $25,000 reward has never been claimed, and they encourage anyone with information to come forward.

Aside from the obvious question of "Who did it?" the one question surrounding the Burger Chef case is why it's such a hard case to resolve. While it is easy to point out the mistakes made early in the investigation, the limitations of late 1970s forensic technology and the publicity surrounding the case that handicapped the agencies that put in countless man-hours looking into the quadruple homicide in hopes of bringing those responsible to justice, it also discounts the real reason the perpetrators were able to commit the "perfect crime." Every once in a while, everything lines up so well that the criminal is able to get away with something. Sometimes the crime is executed perfectly, sometimes there are investigative errors and sometimes it's just dumb luck that helps the criminal to evade the long arm of the law.

The Burger Chef murders are a combination of all three. The perpetrators planned a quick and easy restaurant robbery using a proven method to get ahold of some quick cash. When the police were called in to investigate, they mistakenly thought it might be an inside job and were less than proactive in those first critical hours. And then the what ifs: If authorities had not allowed the restaurant to be cleaned of any latent evidence that might have been on the premises, authorities might have had more to work with. If the identity of one of the perpetrators was not known to at least one of the employees (as alleged), perhaps the robbery would not have turned to murder. If Mark Flemmonds had only fallen in a different direction, he might have lived to tell the police what happened. If only…hindsight isn't 20/20.

They say that history does not always repeat itself, but it often rhymes, and in spite of the advances that have been made in investigative technology, crimes that resemble the Burger Chef murder mystery in some form or another continue to occur. Here are just a few other notable Indiana cases that remain open investigations.

A FAMILY'S NIGHTMARE

On March 27, 1986, eighteen-year-old Denise Pflum left her parents' home in Everton to attend a nearby house party. The following day, the Connersville High School senior realized she'd left her purse behind. She called several friends and asked them to go with her in order to retrieve it, but everyone was busy, and she had to go alone. She was never seen or heard from again.

The family's cream-colored Buick Regal, which Denise drove to collect her purse, was discovered on March 29 a half mile off State Road 44 near Glenwood on the Rush/Fayette County line. The car was locked, and there were no signs of a struggle. Subsequent investigation revealed no other evidence. Denise's purse was at the house where she left it, implying that she never arrived at her intended destination.

At first, it appeared like an open-and-shut case: Denise ran away from home. However, that didn't satisfy Denise's parents, David and Judith Pflum. They knew their daughter to be an honor student, an athlete and a young woman only two months away from her high school graduation. In fact, she had recently chosen her prom dress and had been accepted to Miami University in Oxford, Ohio, where she planned to major in microbiology. While it's true that Denise and her boyfriend had split up not that long before, the pair parted on friendly terms, and there was no reason to suspect that he had a motive in her disappearance.

At five feet tall and 135 pounds, Denise left home wearing a Mötley Crüe T-shirt, a pair of striped jeans and white sneakers. After news of her disappearance was made public, the Fayette County Sheriff's Department received several tips of possible sightings, but none of the calls led to the missing girl.

In 2007, Indiana State Police detective Scott Jarvis was assigned to the Pflum case. Over the years, there were a number of theories that emerged to explain the vanishing of Denise Pflum, who only wanted to collect her purse and go home. Some say she may have walked in on something she shouldn't have seen, such as a drug deal, while others said something went wrong on her way to the farmhouse. Still others say they think they know where Denise's remains may be buried.

"So far, there is not one constant theory," Jarvis said in 2014. "There isn't anybody we have focused on or any person of interest."

Like the Burger Chef murders, the disappearance of Denise Pflum thirty-two years ago is one that features a young person who went missing under mysterious circumstances. It involves a young woman who, by all appearances, had everything going for her and did not have any enemies. It is also plagued by the problem of time. "Anytime this much time goes by, any potential witnesses could have died or moved on," Jarvis said. "The longer this goes on, the more rumors that can come about."

If you have any information about the Denise Pflum case, contact the Indiana State Police Investigative Commander at 1-800-527-4752.

A CAMPUS CASUALTY?

Lauren Spierer was a petite and vivacious twenty-year-old blond sophomore at Indiana University's Bloomington campus when she disappeared in the early morning hours of June 2, 2011.

According to eyewitness accounts, as well as surveillance footage, at 2:30 a.m., Lauren arrived at Kilroy's Sports Bar with her friend Corey Rossman only to leave approximately thirty minutes later, leaving her shoes and cellphone behind. The pair then made their way to Spierer's Smallwood Plaza apartment about a block away from the popular bar. They rode the elevator to the fifth floor, and when the doors opened, they encountered four young men who didn't like the look of the situation. Lauren appeared to be visibly out of it, and they got into an argument with Rossman, who ultimately hit one of the guys in the face.

At 3:00 a.m., Lauren and Rossman left the apartment building and took a deserted alleyway toward Rossman's apartment complex at 11th and Morton Streets. Along the way, Lauren fell twice, causing Rossman to pick her up, in what is known as a "fireman's carry," and take her to his place. Police would later find Lauren's keys and a small purse she used in the alley.

Once home, Rossman got sick and went to bed. His roommate took Lauren to Jay Rosenbaum's apartment, which was about thirty feet away. Rosenbaum saw the condition Lauren was in and suggested that she stay on his couch to "sleep it off," but Lauren refused. At 4:30 a.m., she said she wanted to go home. Rosenbaum said he accompanied her for about a block and then watched as she continued alone. She was last seen at the corner of College Avenue and 11th Street—about two or three blocks from her apartment.

The following day, Lauren's boyfriend, Jesse Wolff, texted her cellphone. Lauren didn't answer, but a bar employee did and told him that the phone had been left behind. He immediately contacted the police and filed a missing person's report. Lauren's parents, Charlene and Robert Spierer, were told of their daughter's disappearance later that day.

The case made headlines and was featured on the local and national news. It was also shared across social media. Volunteers set out to search dumpsters across Bloomington, dense forests and lakeside inlets—anywhere Lauren might be. Police examined the timeline, as well as the corroborating video evidence, and said that the entire known crime scene is focused on a very small geographic area. While they did not rule out a random act of violence, it seemed unlikely that Lauren disappeared at the hands of a complete stranger, and the "friends" she was with that night remain people of interest.

Similar to the Burger Chef murders, the Lauren Spierer case was heavily publicized, which caused tips to flood into the Bloomington Police Department. Within two weeks of the coed's disappearance, investigators received more than one thousand tips. Those tips led police to discover a darker side to Lauren's college experience; they looked into ex-convicts in white trucks, a motorcycle club "enforcer" and a former IU student named Corey Hammersley who, like Lauren, got involved in the school's party and drug scene.

In 2012, Hammersley was involved in an incident that led to a twenty-four-year prison sentence, and during a card game with another inmate, he allegedly confessed to knowing what happened to Lauren. He claimed that she had accidentally overdosed on the night of her disappearance. Those who were with her got scared, and because they didn't know what to do, they took her to the Ohio River and dumped her body in the water. (As of this writing, there is no evidence to suggest Lauren's body is in the river.)

Former FBI investigator Brad Garrett said it is a plausible explanation. "The idea is very simple. One of the mistakes in most criminal cases is we, investigators, try to make them too complicated. And many times, at the end of the day, they end up being quite simple. The simplest is, she died at a party and somebody got rid of her."

Seven years after their daughter's disappearance, Lauren's parents vowed to keep searching for answers. The family shared a note on their Facebook page to assure the public that they continue to hold out hope, and their quest to find out what happened to their daughter is far from over.

"Lauren's disappearance has been and continues to be the most heart wrenching experience of our lives. Seven years later, we continue our search for Lauren, for truth, for justice. Our sincerest of thanks to those who have stood by our sides since June 3, 2011 and who continue to do so."

If you have any information on the disappearance of Lauren Spierer, contact the Bloomington Police Department at (812) 339-4477.

The Snapchat Murders

If there is one case that resembles the Burger Chef murders in terms of its apparent randomness, it is the shocking deaths of Liberty "Libby" German, fourteen, and Abigail "Abby" Williams, thirteen, of Delphi.

On February 13, 2017, the two eighth graders went for a walk on an unseasonably warm winter day along the Delphi Historic Trails. The girls were dropped off at approximately 1:00 p.m. and arranged to meet relatives at the start of the trail an hour later. As they walked along, the girls posted photos of their "make up snow day" adventure to their social media accounts. Shortly before 2:15 p.m., Libby posted a photo to Snapchat of Abby walking on the Monon High railroad bridge.

Around 3:00 p.m., a family member texted Libby's phone to tell the teenager that they were on their way to pick up the girls, but there was no response. There were also no girls waiting for them at the pickup location. More texts were sent and calls made, but they all went unanswered. Something was definitely wrong.

Friends and family members organized themselves into search parties to look for Libby and Abby. They set out on the trail, crossed the abandoned rail trestle and scoured the woods lining Deer Creek. However, it wasn't until noon the following day that a group of volunteers located the bodies of the two girls a half mile from the bridge where Libby took the now infamous Snapchat photo. Evidence was collected at the crime scene and autopsies were performed, but the nature of the evidence and the cause of death have never been revealed.

Investigators believe that while on their walk, Libby and Abby were approached by a man wearing blue jeans, a brown hoodie, a navy blue jacket and a black "cabbie" hat. This man was responsible for killing them. They assume the man was not known to the girls prior to their encounter, and police believe that Libby might have sensed there was danger nearby when she took at least two pictures of the stranger and recorded an audio clip on her cellphone in which a man can be heard saying "down the hill." Police believe that the voice on the recording belongs to the man in the blurry photo and that he is their prime suspect.

The suspect is described as a white male with reddish-brown hair between five feet six inches and five feet ten inches tall with a weight between 180 and 220 pounds. Police have not confirmed or denied the existence of additional photos, video or audio recordings on Libby's phone but hailed the girl as a hero for getting the photos and audio she did before her death. Investigators feel it is important to protect the integrity of their investigation by not showing their entire hand, which, as the Burger Chef case shows, can lead to challenging results.

"There are certain people that know the details and if we release it all, then we get into false confessions," said Indiana State Police first sergeant Jerry Holeman, investigative commander for the Lafayette District.

In the eighteen months since the Delphi murders, authorities have received more than thirty-five thousand tips from the public. In September 2017, investigators named Daniel Nations as a person of interest in the case. Nations was a registered sex offender who used to live in Indiana and was arrested in Colorado for threatening people with a hatchet along a hiking trail. These incidents occurred around the same time that a cyclist was fatally shot on the trail. According to an El Paso County sheriff's official, there were a number of similarities in the cases, but by February 2018, Indiana State Police announced they were no longer looking at Nations as a possible suspect.

Authorities have stated unequivocally that they are determined not to let the Delphi case grow cold. No doubt memories of the Spierer case, the Pflum disappearance and the Burger Chef murders factor in a case of this nature, but authorities say things aren't always as they appear.

"I've said all along, as long as I am in this role and breathing, we're not leaving the City of Dephi in Carroll County, Indiana, we're just not," said Indiana State Police superintendent Doug Carter. "If we get to the point where we have exhausted the leads in the queue then we're going to start all over again."

As of this writing, no one has been charged in the crime. Anyone with information regarding the Delphi murder case is encouraged to contact the authorities by calling the tip line at 1-844-459-5786 or via e-mail at abbyandlibbytip@cacoshrf.com.

The Truth Is Out There

No matter how much time has passed, whether it is one month, one year, one decade or, in the case of the Burger Chef murders, nearly a half century, one thing is certain: the truth is out there. Here is hoping that the truth comes to light sooner rather than later for the victims, their families and the people who love them, and that justice is served once and for all.

BIBLIOGRAPHY

Anderson, Terry. "Clue Search Continues." *Daily Journal*, November 24, 1978. www.newspapers.com/image/154789614.

Anderson, Terry, and Sally King. "Few Solid Leads." *Daily Journal*, November 22, 1978, 1. www.newspapers.com/image/154789495/?terms=we%27ve+got+to+hope+that+the+killer+or+killers.

Anderson, William. "No Censorship Says Johnson Prosecutor Gantz." *Indianapolis Star*, November 22, 1978, 7. www.newspapers.com/image/106963126.

AP. "Burger Chef Killings—One Year Later." *Call-Leader*, November 19, 1979, 1, 3. www.newspapers.com/image/90226628.

———. "Speedway Probe Continues." *Call-Leader*, November 25, 1978. www.newspapers.com/image/88796930/?terms=Robert%2BFlemmonds.

Barcella, Laura. "The Unsolved Delphi Murders: What Happened to Indiana Teens Libby German and Abby Williams?" A&E, n.d. www.aetv.com/real-crime/the-unsolved-delphi-murders-what-happened-to-indiana-teens-libby-german-and-abby-williams.

Beaven, Stephen. "Burger Chef Killings Still a Haunting Dead End." *Indianapolis Star*, November 15, 1998, A1, A12. www.newspapers.com/image/107291544.

Beringer, Erica. "Headstone Donated for Burger Chef Victim." WISHTV.com, January 19, 2015. www.wishtv.com/news/local-news/headstone-donated-for-burger-chef-murder-victim/1115218606.

Bird, Paul. "Burger Chef Slayings Data Checked Daily." *Indianapolis News*, July 25, 1980, 28. www.newspapers.com/image/312680630/?terms=I%2Bfeel%2Bin%2Bmy%2Bheart%2Bthat%2Bwe%2Bwill%2Bsolve%2Bthis%2Bcase.

Corbin, Bryan. "Burger Chef Case Never Explained." *Daily Journal*, June 28, 2003, 1–2. www.newspapers.com/image/158223457.

————. "Parents Mourn Life that Ended Too Soon." *Daily Journal*, November 27, 1993, 1, 6. www.newspapers.com/image/155160063.

————. "Unsolved but Not Forgotten." *Daily Journal*, November 27, 1993, 1, 6. www.newspapers.com/image/155160063.

Daily Journal. "Site Search Reveals No New Information." November 27, 1978, 1, 14. www.newspapers.com/image/154789755.

Davis, Chris. "The Burger Chef Murders: 40 Years of Evidence Includes the Knife." WIBC, November 14, 2018. www.wibc.com/news/local-news/burger-chef-murders-40-years-evidence-includes-knife.

————. "Indiana Cold Case: The Burger Chef Murders." WIBC, May 24, 2018. www.wibc.com/news/local-news/indiana-cold-case-burger-chef-murders.

Ellis, Mike. "Shootings Frighten Rural Residents." *Indianapolis News*, November 20, 1978, 12. www.newspapers.com/image/312819885/?terms=Cheryl%2BGerdt.

Frederick, Diane. "Lights to 'Happy Face' Turned Off." *Indianapolis News*, November 21, 1978, P20. www.newspapers.com/image/312821483/?terms=Students%2B yesterday%2Bwere%2Ball%2Bday%2Blong%2Bvery%2Bquiet%2C%2Bthere %2Bwas%2Bsome%2Bdiscussion%2Babout%2Bit%2B(the%2Bkilling).

Galer, Sara. "Unsolved: Burger Chef Murders." WTHR 13, November 14, 2013. www.wthr.com/article/unsolved-burger-chef-murders.

Gelarden, Joseph. "Three Victims of Senseless Burger Chef Slaying Buried." *Indianapolis Star*, November 23, 1978, P6. www.newspapers.com/image/106963354.

Gelarden, Joseph, and Patrick Morrison. "2 Suspects in Murders Named." *Indianapolis Star*, December 13, 1978, P1. www.newspapers.com/image/106966196.

Guerra, Kristine. "Indiana Missing: Connersville Teen Vanished in 1986." *Indianapolis Star*, March 2, 2014, A23. www.newspapers.com/image/106596002 /?terms=Connersville%2BTeen%2Bvanished.

Hess, Skip. "The Mystery Lingers." *Indianapolis News*, November 13, 1993, P1-2. www.newspapers.com/image/313301568.

Higgins, Will. "Burger Chef Murders Case Still Open—Debated." *Indianapolis Star*, November 20, 2017, A1, 17–19. www.newspapers.com/image/355347185.

————. "Here's Why Police Think a Photo of a Knife Might Help Them Solve the Burger Chef Murders." *Indianapolis Star*, November 14, 2018. www.indystar. com/story/entertainment/2018/11/15/burger-chef-murders-indianapolis-investigation-40-years/1989846002.

Indianapolis News. "Burger Chef Suspect Says He's Innocent, Wants Trial." December 19, 1986, 35. www.newspapers.com/image/312864753/?terms=I%27ve%2Bne ver%2Bsigned%2Bone%2Bof%2Bthose%2Bin%2Bmy%2Blife.

———. "Services Difficult to Prepare, Deliver." November 22, 1978, 20. www. newspapers.com/image/312822508/?terms=That%2Bimpressed%2Bme%2B almost%2Bmore%2Bthan%2Banything%2C%22%2BBlowers%2Bsaid.

Indianapolis Star. "Burger Chef, Scyphers Killing, Bombings: Seek Ties in Speedway Murders." March 1, 1979, 1, 15. www.newspapers.com/image/106978170.

———. "Killers Psyches May Be Sketched." December 22, 1978, 1, 14. www. newspapers.com/image/106179823.

———. "Mayor Pleads to Persons Who Know about Murders to Offer Information." December 9, 1978, P1. www.newspapers.com/image/106964151.

———. "Murder Investigators Get 16 More Letters." November 27, 1978, 1. www. newspapers.com/image/106966277.

———. "Reward Fund Donations Refused by Burger Chef." November 23, 1978, 6. www.newspapers.com/image/106963354.

———. "Some in Speedway Talk of Moving Out." November 21, 1978, 8. www. newspapers.com/image/106962941.

———. "Someone in This City Knows Who Killed Four Employees." December 7, 1978, 9. www.newspapers.com/image/106963344.

———. "Star Getting Useful Letters from Public on Speedway Slayings." November 29, 1978, 1, 10. www.newspapers.com/image/106966754.

———. "They Could Have Been Anyone's Children." November 21, 1978. www. newspapers.com/image/106962941.

———. "Tip Involves Trio in Murders." December 15, 1978, 1. www.newspapers. com/image/106966865.

Jachimiak, Jim. "Detectives: Errors Hurt Investigation." *Daily Journal*, November 17, 1988, 6. www.newspapers.com/image/154878563/?terms=Burger%2BChe f%2Bmurders%2Btoo%2Bmany%2Bchiefs.

———. "Murders Still a Mystery 10 Years Later." *Daily Journal*, November 17, 1988, 1, 6. www.newspapers.com/image/154878505/?terms=Probably%2Bm ost%2Bof%2Bthe%2Bleads%2Bwe%2Bget%2Bare%2Bfrom%2Bconvicts%2B or%2Bex-convicts%2C%2Bbut%2Bother%2Bthan%2Bthat%2C%2Bthere%2 Bare%2Bno%2Bsolid%2Bleads%2Bcoming%2Bin.

Judkins, Jane. "Young Speedway Murder Victims." *Indianapolis News*, November 20, 1978, 1. www.newspapers.com/image/312819589/?terms=they%2Bwere%2Bs tudying%2Bthe%2Bbook%2Bof%2Brevelation%2Band%2Bshe%2Bwas%2Bre ally%2Bfascinated%2Bby%2Bthat.

Keating, Thomas. "Let Your Children Work, Mrs. Friedt Says to Parents." *Indianapolis Star*, December 3, 1978, section 5, 1. www.newspapers.com/image/106962142.

———. "Subconscious Aids Police." *Indianapolis Star*, November 23, 1978, 25. www. newspapers.com/image/106963443.

———. "Victims Were Exceptional." *Indianapolis Star*, November 21, 1978, 21. www.newspapers.com/image/106962997.

King, Sally. "Burger Chef Murder Suspect May Have Johnson County Tie." *Daily Journal*, October 9, 1980, 1, 18. www.newspapers.com/image/154760676/?terms=To%2Bme%2C%2BI%2Balways%2Bthought%2Bsomeone%2Bhad%2Bto%2Bknow%2Bwhere%2Bthat%2Bplace%2Bwas.%2BThey%2Bdidn%27t%2Bjust%2Bstumble%2Bacross%2Bit%2C%22%2Bhe%2Bsaid.%2B%22I%2Bwas%2Balways%2Bworking%2Bon%2Bthe%2Btheory%2Bthat%2Bit%2Bhad%2Bto%2Bbe%2Bsomeone%2Bwith%2BJohnson%2BCounty%2Bties.%22.

———. "New Information Revealed on Burger Chef Case." *Daily Journal*, January 4, 1980, 1. www.newspapers.com/image/154816695/?terms=Gantz+Burger+Chef+I+didn%27t+think+I+could+rule+them+out+as+suspects.

———. "Police Still Seek Burger Chef Clues." *Daily Journal*, November 17, 1980, P1. www.newspapers.com/image/154748916/?terms=%22We%2Bintend%2Bto%2Bkeep%2Bworking%2Bon%2Bthis.%2BWe%27re%2Bstill%2Bpushing.

King, Sally, and Terry Anderson. "Authorities Sift Murder Clues." *Daily Journal*, November 21, 1978, 1, 12. www.newspapers.com/image/154789458.

———. "Local Search Continues after Four Found Dead in County." *Daily Journal*, November 20, 1978, 1, 14. www.newspapers.com/image/154789390.

Konz, Joseph. "Burger Chef Arrest Expected." *Indianapolis Star*, October 9, 1980, 1. www.newspapers.com/image/107630332/?terms=We%2Bknow%2Bwho%2Bone%2B(of%2Bthe%2Bmurderers)%2Bwas%2C%22%2Bhe%2Bsaid.%2B%22I%2Bhave%2Bno%2Bdoubts%2Bin%2Bmy%2Bmind%2Bthe%2Bsuspect%2Bcan%2Bbe%2Bplaced%2Bin%2Bthe%2Bwoods%2Bin%2BJohnson%2BCounty%2Bat%2Bthe%2Btime%2Bof%2Bthe%2Bmurders.%22.

Lewbell, Paris, and Katie Cox. "Delphi Investigation: Why State Police Say Libby and Abby's Case Isn't Cold." WRTV, February 12, 2018. www.theindychannel.com/longform/delphi-investigation-why-state-police-say-libby-abbys-case-isnt-cold.

Luzadder, Dan. "Burger Chef Break Follows 2-Year Odyssey." *Indianapolis Star*, November 16, 1986, 1, 30. www.newspapers.com/image/105894791/?terms=Burger%2BChef%2Bbreak%2Bfollows%2B2-year%2Bodyssey.

———. "Burger Chef 'Revelations' Lock Inmate in Loneliness." *Indianapolis Star*, November 19, 1988, 1, 8. www.newspapers.com/image/105948316/?terms=Burger%2BChef%2Brevelations%2Block%2Binmate%2Bin%2Bloneliness.

———. "Charges against Forrester Planned." *Indianapolis Star*, November 19, 1986, 1, 10. www.newspapers.com/image/105902318/?terms=Charges%2Bagainst%2BForrester%2Bplanned.

———. "Conflicts, Lies Mar Burger Chef Case." *Indianapolis Star*, November 17, 1986, 1, 8. www.newspapers.com/image/105899371/?terms=Conflicts%2C%2Blies%2Bmar%2BBurger%2BChef%2Bcase.

———. "Forrester Won't Be Charged in '78 Killings." *Indianapolis Star*, December 23, 1986, 1, 6. www.newspapers.com/image/106239146/?terms=Forrester%2Bwon%27t%2Bbe%2Bcharged%2Bin%2B%2778%2Bkillings.

Luzadder, Dan, and George McLaren. "Burger Chef Suspect Recants, Denies Slayings." *Indianapolis Star*, November 18, 1986, 1, 8. www.newspapers.com/image/105900156/?terms=Burger%2BChef%2Bsuspect%2Bdenies%2Bslayings.

Mack, Justin. "Lauren Spierer Case: Family Vows to Keep Looking 7 Years after Disappearance." *Indianapolis Star*, June 4, 2018. www.indystar.com/story/news/fox59/2018/06/04/missing-indiana-university-student-lauren-spierer-disappeared-7-years-ago/668542002.

McLayea, Eunice, and Patrick Morrison. "Junkies May Have Slain Burger Chef Employees." *Indianapolis Star*, January 3, 1979, 1, 4. www.newspapers.com/image/106961503/?terms=Indianapolis%2BStar.

Miley, Scott. "Jailed Man Waits Questioning in Burger Chef Case." *Indianapolis Star*, March 19, 1981, 50. www.newspapers.com/image/106122925/?terms=James%2BFriedt%2Bmarijuana.

Morrison, Patrick. "Prisoner Knows More Than Most about the Murder of 4, Test Shows." *Indianapolis Star*, January 30, 1979, 1, 5. www.newspapers.com/image/106971827.

———. "Revelations in Burger Chef Case Bring Mixed Emotions." *Indianapolis Star*, November 16, 1986, 30. www.newspapers.com/image/105895380/?terms=Burger%2BChef.

———. "Victim Parents Appeal for Murder Data." *Indianapolis Star*, December 17, 1978, 1, 22. www.newspapers.com/image/106171007.

Morrison, Patrick T., and James G. Newland. "Kidnap Victims Believed Slain by More Than One." *Indianapolis Star*, November 21, 1978, 1, 8. www.newspapers.com/image/106962907.

Newland, James. "Clay Busts Made of Two Men Sought in Speedway Slayings." *Indianapolis Star*, November 25, 1978, 1, 18. www.newspapers.com/image/106964583.

Nichols, Mark. "Painful Memories of 1978 Murders Remain with Families." *Indianapolis Star*, November 15, 1986, 12. www.newspapers.com/image/105900438/?terms=Robert%2BFlemmonds.

O'Neal, Kevin. "The Burger Chef Murders: 25 Years Later Police No Closer to Solving the Mystery." *Indianapolis Star*, November 17, 2003, 1, 8. www.newspapers.com/image/127309756/?terms=The%2BBurger%2BChef%2Bmurders%2B25%2Byears%2Blater.

Richardson, Joan. "Speedway Police Chief Copeland Fired." *Indianapolis Star*, October 3, 1979, 15. www.newspapers.com/image/107224438.

Ross, Brian, and Brian Epstein. "5 Years after She Vanished, New Hope in Lauren Spierer Sase." ABC News, June 24, 2016. abcnews.go.com/US/lauren-spierer-case-years-vanished-hope/story?id=40084230.

Runevitch, Jennie. "Police Release Evidence in Burger Chef Cold Case Murders 40 Years Later." WTHR, November 14, 2018. www.wthr.com/article/police-release-evidence-burger-chef-cold-case-murders-40-years-later.

Shelton, Rachel. Excerpts from her diary appeared in the November 27, 1993 edition of the *Daily Journal*, 12. www.newspapers.com/image/155160074.

Sylvester, Rosemary. "Burger Chef Case Still Baffling." *Daily Journal*, November 18, 1987, 3. www.newspapers.com/image/154825452/?terms=Officials%2Bunsure%2Bthey%27ll%2Bever%2Blocate%2Bthe%2Bmurderer.

———. "Confession Confuses Probe." *Daily Journal*, November 18, 1987, 3. www.newspapers.com/image/154825452/?terms=Confession%2Bconfuses%2Bprobe.%22.

———. "Forrester Remains a Puzzling Character." *Daily Journal*, November 17, 1988, 6. www.newspapers.com/image/154878563/?terms=Forrester%2Bremains%2Ba%2Bpuzzling%2Bcharacter.

———. "Police Try to Link Forrester's Cases." *Daily Journal*, January 19, 1987, 3. www.newspapers.com/image/154872237/?terms=We%2Bcouldn%27t%2Bmake%2Bheads%2Bor%2Btails%2Bout%2Bof%2Bit%2Band%2Bthe%2Bproblem%2Bwas%2Bthat%2Bmost%2Bof%2Bthe%2Brecords%2Bwere%2Bexpunged%2Bbecause%2Bthe%2Bvictim%2Bwas%2Ba%2Bjuvenile.

———. "Victims' Families Trying to Move Ahead." *Daily Journal*, November 17, 1988, 6. www.newspapers.com/image/154878563.

Thrasher, Donald. "Kidnap-Murder Victim's Father Not Bitter; Talks Love, Hope." *Indianapolis Star*, November 24, 1978, 10. www.newspapers.com/image/106964260.

UPI. "Slayings: Police Checking Leads No Matter How Far Away." *Daily Journal*, November 29, 1978, 1. www.newspapers.com/image/154789828/?terms=.

Walton, Richard. "Inmate of Ohio Jail 'Good Suspect' in Kidnap Killings." *Indianapolis Star*, December 3, 1978, 1, 22. www.newspapers.com/image/106961613.

———. "Police Baffled by Kidnappings." *Indianapolis Star*, November 19, 1978, A1, 12. www.newspapers.com/image/106961660.

Walton, Richard, Ernest Wilkinson and Mike McNamee. "3 Explosions Rock Speedway." *Indianapolis Star*, September 2, 1978, 1, 12. www.newspapers.com/image/106954380/?terms=Speedway%2Bpolice%2Bcpl.%2BGary%2BDonaldson.

Witkin, Gordon. "Burger Chef Employee's Death Resulted from Blows to Head." *Indianapolis Star*, December 11, 1978, P1. www.newspapers.com/image/106965704.

Zabarenko, D. "A Year Later, Burger Chef Slayings Remain a Mystery." *Palladium-Item*, November 19, 1979, 10. www.newspapers.com/image/251147196/?terms=Zabarenko,+D.+Palladium-Item.

ABOUT THE AUTHOR

J ulie Young is an award-winning writer and author who has written several books on Indiana history, including *Famous Faces of WTTV-4*, *Eastside Indianapolis: A Brief History*, *CYO in Indianapolis and Central Indiana* and *Historic Irvington*. She is also the author of two books for the Idiot's Guide series and the YA novel *Fifteen Minutes of Fame*. She lives near Indianapolis with her family.